Anonymous

Christian Science Hymnal

A Selection of spiritual songs

Anonymous

Christian Science Hymnal
A Selection of spiritual songs

ISBN/EAN: 9783337181499

Printed in Europe, USA, Canada, Australia, Japan

Cover: Foto ©Lupo / pixelio.de

More available books at **www.hansebooks.com**

CHRISTIAN SCIENCE HYMNAL

A SELECTION OF

SPIRITUAL SONGS

PUBLISHED BY
CHRISTIAN SCIENCE PUBLISHING SOCIETY
BOSTON, MASS.
1898

PREFACE TO REVISED HYMNAL.

In presenting this Revised Hymnal the committee do not claim that it is strictly scientific, as they were obliged to select very largely from hymns composed by those who were unacquainted with the teachings of Christian Science. While not entirely composed of hymns written exactly in accordance with the doctrines of Christian Science, it presents the acme of religious and poetic thought contained in the best hymns of the day, as well as in the best compositions thus far contributed by Christian Scientists.

Much labor has been bestowed upon this compilation by the Committee, and in the musical department of this work great credit is due Mr. Lyman Brackett of Boston, Mass., for untiring effort to present the most useful and varied collection of tunes ever issued in one hymnal,—the purpose being to appeal to every lover of church music, of whatever taste or ability. Special attention has been given to the wedding of words and music, not only as to character of composition, but in respect to proper accentuation, etc., wherever it has been found possible.

The Revision of the Christian Science Hymnal has been made with a view to eliminate the difficulties which many users of the book have found in connecting the proper words or syllables of hymns with their corresponding notes in either of the three tunes as used in the former arrangement. To accomplish this purpose it was decided to publish a Hymnal, in which the words and the syllables shall appear beneath the notes to which they are to be sung.

In revising the hymnal it was found impracticable to use all the music in the old Hymnal, as the new book would comprise nearly 700 pages and the cost would be largely increased. It has therefore been the aim of the Committee to select for this Hymnal the music that is the best known and the most used.

In every case the first hymn has been set to the first tune with the exception of No. 47. The second hymns have been set either to the second or the third

CHRISTIAN SCIENCE HYMNAL.

tunes to which they have been formerly sung with the exceptions of hymns 12, 16, 18, 34, 38, 48, 52, 54, 58, 64, 76, 82, 90, 106, 114, 118, which have been set to other second or third tunes, for the reason that some of the second tunes — old German and English chorals — seem to find but little favor with the general modern taste, and some of the third tunes written for solos are not well adapted for congregational singing.

The tunes from 1 to 179 have been selected especially with a view to their adaptability for congregational singing. Some of the best known and favorite hymns, "Abide with me," "Onward, Christian Soldiers," "Still, still with Thee," "Lead, kindly Light," "Shepherd, show me how to go," "O'er waiting harp-strings," "Saw ye my Saviour," and a few others have received duplicate settings and are placed in the latter part of the book. In addition to these hymns two others, "I need Thee every hour" and "I'm a pilgrim and I'm a stranger," have been added at the suggestion of the Rev. Mary Baker Eddy. There will be found, also, a new setting of "O'er waiting harp-strings of the mind" to one of Mr. Brackett's best tunes.

Acknowledgments are due to Oliver Ditson Co., C. H. Richards, The Century Co., American Unitarian Association, Methodist Book Concern, Anson D. F. Randolph & Co., A. S. Barnes & Co., J. & A. McMillan, Fillmore Bros., and others, for use of hymns published by them.

Boston, Mass., 1897.

CHRISTIAN SCIENCE HYMNAL

1 Old Hundred. L. M.

Isaac Watts, alt. Guillaume Franck.

2 I Praise Thee, Lord, for Blessings Sent. L. M.

Brackett.

1. I praise Thee, Lord, for bless-ings sent To break the dream of hu-man power. For now my shal-low cis-tern's spent, I find Thy font and thirst no more.
2. I take Thy hand and fears grow still; Be-hold Thy face, and doubts re-move; Who would not yield his wav-'ring will To per-fect truth and bound-less love!
3. That truth gives prom-ise of a dawn, Be-neath whose light I am to see, When all these blind-ing vails are drawn, This was the wis-est path for me.

4 Press On, Press On, Ye Sons of Light. L. M.

William Gaskell.   Brackett.

1. Press on, press on! ye sons of light,
Un-tir-ing in your ho-ly fight,
Still tread-ing each temp-ta-tion down,
And bat-tling for a bright-er crown.

2. Press on, press on! still look in faith
To him who con-q'reth sin and death:
Then shall ye hear his word, "Well done."
True to the last, press on, press on!

6 Kingdoms and Thrones to God Belong. L. M.

Isaac Watts, abr.   Brackett.

1. Kingdoms and thrones to God belong;
   Crown Him, ye nations, in your song;
   His wondrous name and pow'r rehearse;
   His honors shall enrich your verse.

2. Proclaim Him King, pronounce Him blest;
   He's your defence, your joy, your rest;
   When terrors rise, and nations faint,
   God is the strength of ev'ry saint.

7 Germany. L. M.

Mrs. Livermore, abr. — Beethoven.

1. Je - sus, what pre - cept is like thine, "For - give, as ye would be for-giv'n!" If heed - ed, O what pow'r di - vine Would then trans-form our earth to heav'n.
2. Not by the harsh or scorn - ful word, Should we our broth - er seek to gain; Not by the pris - on or the sword, The shack - le, or the clank-ing chain.
3. But from our hearts must ev - er flow A love that will his wrong out-weigh; Our lips must on - ly bless-ings know, And wrath, and sin shall die a - way.

8 Sun of Our Life, Thy Quickening Ray. L. M.

Oliver Wendell Holmes, abr. — Brackett.

1. Sun of our life, Thy quick-'ning ray
Sheds on our path the glow of day;
Star of our hope, Thy soft-ened light
Cheers the long watches of the night.

2. Lord of all life, be-low, a-bove,
Whose light is truth, whose warmth is love,
Be-fore Thy ev-er-blaz-ing throne
We ask no lus-tre of our own.

3. Grant us Thy truth to make us free,
And kin-dling hearts that burn for Thee,
Till all Thy liv-ing al-tars claim
One ho-ly light, one heav'n-ly flame.

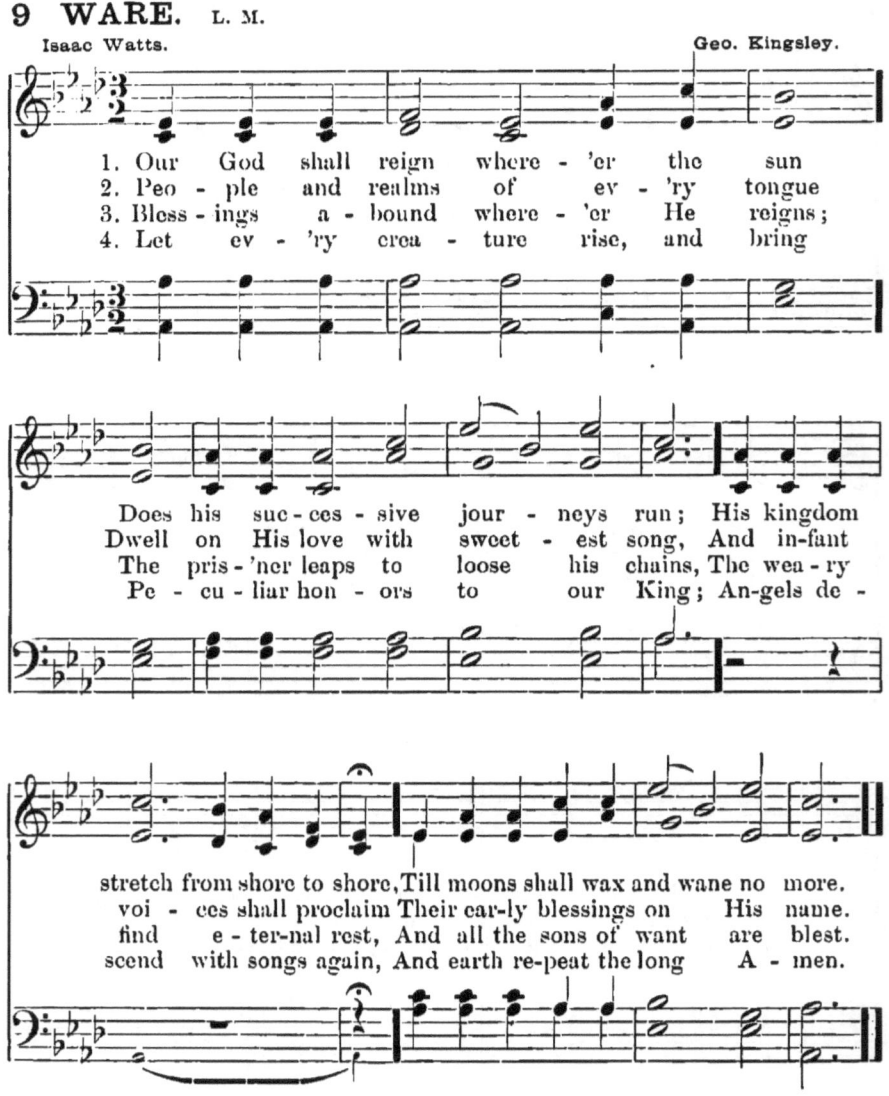

10 Father, Thou Joy of Loving Hearts. L. M.

Ray Palmer, tr.   Brackett.

1. Father, Thou Joy of loving hearts,
2. Thy truth unchanged hath ever stood;

Thou Fount of life! Thou Light of men! From the best
Thou savest those that on Thee call; To them that

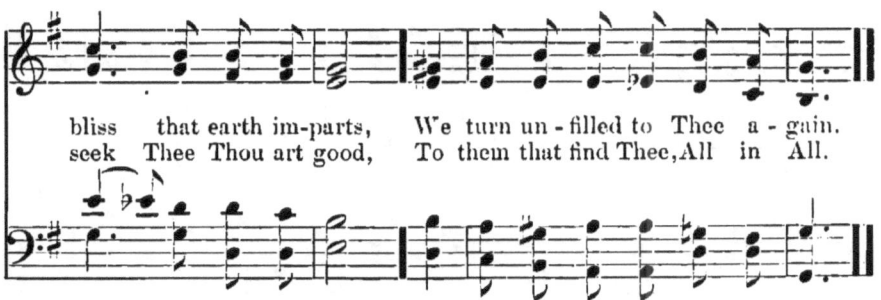

bliss that earth imparts, We turn unfilled to Thee again.
seek Thee Thou art good, To them that find Thee, All in All.

12 Lord, May Thy Truth upon the Heart. L. M.

Caroline Gilman. Schumann.

1. Lord, may Thy truth upon the heart Now fall and dwell as heav'n-ly dew, And flow'rs of grace in fresh-ness start Where once the weeds of er-ror grew!

2. May pray'r now lift her sa-cred wings, Con-tent-ed with that aim a-lone Which bears her to the King of kings, And rests her at His shelt-'ring throne!

14 Had I the Tongues of Greeks and Jews. L. M.

I. Watts, abr.   Brackett.

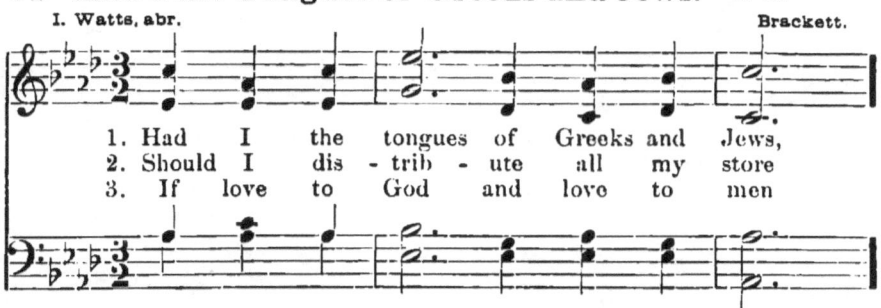

1. Had I the tongues of Greeks and Jews,
2. Should I dis-trib-ute all my store
3. If love to God and love to men

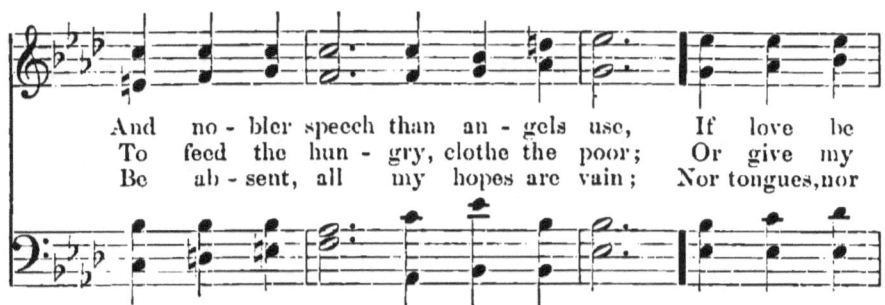

And no-bler speech than an-gels use, If love be
To feed the hun-gry, clothe the poor; Or give my
Be ab-sent, all my hopes are vain; Nor tongues, nor

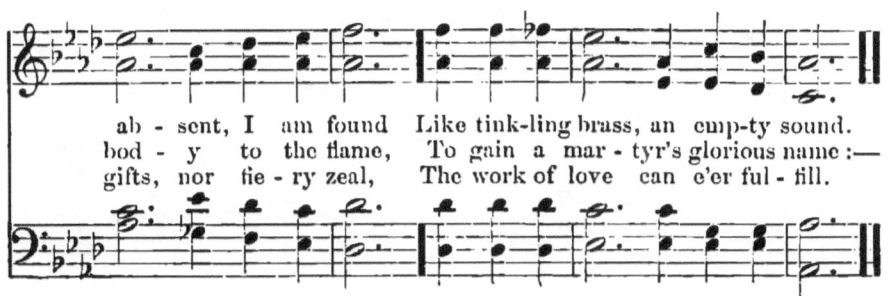

ab - sent, I am found Like tink-ling brass, an emp-ty sound.
bod - y to the flame, To gain a mar - tyr's glorious name:—
gifts, nor fie - ry zeal, The work of love can e'er ful - fill.

15 Zephyr. L. M.

J. Bowring, alt. W. B. Bradbury.

1. Upon the Gospel's sacred page
The gathered beams of ages shine;
And, as it hastens, ev'ry age
But makes its brightness more divine.

2. On mightier wing, in loftier flight,
From year to year does knowledge soar;
And, as it soars, the Gospel light
Becomes effulgent more and more.

3. More glorious still, as centuries roll,
New regions blest, new pow'rs unfurled,
So Truth reveals the perfect whole,
Its radiance shall o'erflow the world,—

4. Flow to restore, but not destroy;
As when the cloudless lamp of day
Pours out its floods of light and joy,
And sweeps the ling'ring mist away.

16 Hath Not Thy Heart within Thee Burned? L. M.

Stephen G. Bulfinch, abr.   Berthold Tours.

1. Hath not thy heart within thee burned
At evening's calm and ho-ly hour, As if its in-most depths discerned The pres-ence of a loft-ier power?

2. It was the voice of God that spake In si-lence to thy si-lent heart; And bade each wor-thier thought a-wake, And ev-'ry dream of earth de-part.

18 Abide Not in the Realm of Dreams. L. M.

William H. Burleigh.
Rev. J. B. Dykes, Mus. Doc.

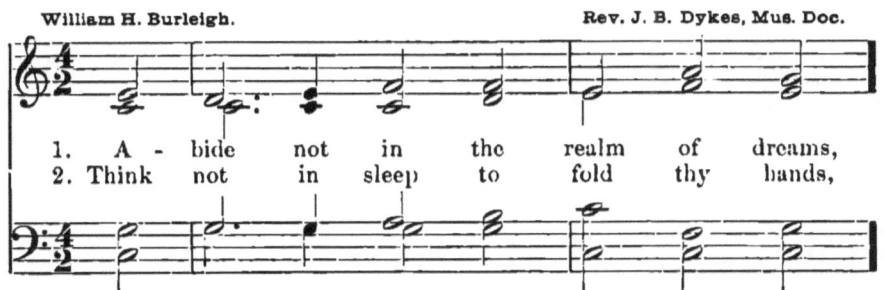

1. A - bide not in the realm of dreams,
2. Think not in sleep to fold thy hands,

O man, how-ev-er fair it seems; But with clear eye the
For - get - ful of thy Lord's com-mands: From du - ty's claims no

pres - ent scan, And hear the call of God and man.
life is free,— Be - hold, to - day hath need of thee!

19 Retreat. L. M.

James Montgomery, alt and abr.
Thomas Hastings.

1. When like a stran-ger on our sphere The low-ly Je-sus wan-dered here, Where-'er He went af-flic-tion fled, The sick were healed, the hun-gry fed.
2. With bound-ing steps the halt and lame, To hail their great De-liv-'rer, came; For him the grave could hold no dread, He spoke the word and raised the dead.
3. Thro' paths of lov-ing kind-ness led Where Je-sus tri-umphed we would tread; To all with will-ing hands dis-pense The gifts of our be-nev-o-lence.

24 Thy Will, Almighty Father, Thine. L. M.

1. Thy will, al - might - y Fa - ther, Thine, And Thine a - lone be ev - er done; For Thou art Life and Truth and Love, The great, e - ter - nal, ho - ly One.
2. Re - flect - ors, we, of all Thou art, Of all the sun-shine of Thy love, No life from Thee we know a - part, But peace on earth of heav'n a - bove.

25 Hursley. L. M.

Cowper, alt.
Francis Joseph Hadyn.
Arr. by William Henry Monk.

1. O Lord! where-'er Thy peo-ple meet, There they be-hold Thy mer-cy-seat; Where-'er they seek Thee, Thou art found, And ev-'ry place is hal-low'd ground.
2. For Thou, with-in no walls con-fined, In-hab-it-est the hum-ble mind; Such ev-er bring Thee where they come, And go-ing, take Thee to their home.
3. Here we may prove the pow'r of pray'r To strengthen faith and sweet-en care; To teach our faint de-sires to rise, And bring all heav'n be-fore our eyes.

26 O God, Whose Presence Glows in All. L. M.

Frothingham, abr.   Brackett.

1. O God, whose pres-ence glows in all,
With-in, a-round us, and a-bove! Thy word we bless, Thy
name we call, Whose word is Truth, whose name is Love.

2. That love its ho-ly in-fluence pour
To keep us meek, and make us free; And throw its bind-ing
bless-ing more Round each with all, and all with Thee.

3. Send down its an-gel to our side,
Send in its calm up-on the breast; For we would know no
oth-er guide; And we can need no oth-er rest.

28 God is the Life, the Truth, the Way. L. M.

Mrs. Keyes. Brackett.

1. God is the Life, the Truth, the Way
Which leads un-to the per-fect day,
The Way which mor-tals should a-dore,
If they would reach the un-seen shore.

2. Come to this fount which flows for all,
Come, and ac-cept the gra-cious call,
Je-sus, who came the Way to show,
Has said, that all, the Way may know.

3. Press for-ward to the Ho-reb height,
Look up and thou shalt see the Light,
Ac-quaint thy-self at once with Love,
And Truth shall guide to Light a-bove.

29 Hamburg. L. M.

Arr. by Lowell Mason.

1. When Jesus, our great Master, came
To teach us in his Father's name, In ev'ry
act, in ev'ry thought, He lived the precepts which he taught.

2. So let our lips and lives express
The holy gospel we profess; So let our
works and virtues shine, To prove the doctrine all divine.

3. Thus shall we best proclaim abroad,
The honors of our Saviour, God, When the salvation reigns within, And grace subdues the claim of sin.

30 If My Immortal Saviour Lives. L. M.

Brackett.

1. If my immortal Saviour lives, Then my immortal life is sure; His word a firm foundation gives; Here may I build, and rest secure.
2. Here let my faith unshaken dwell; For ever sure the promise stands; Not all the claims of earth or hell Can e'er dissolve the sacred bands.
3. Here, O my heart, thy trust repose, If Jesus is forever mine, Not death itself—that last of foes—Shall break a union so divine.

31 Hebron. L. M.

Lowell Mason.

1. The Christian warrior, see him stand In the whole armor of his God; The Spirit's sword is in his hand; His feet are with the gospel shod.
2. In panoply of truth complete, Salvation's helmet on his head, With righteousness, a breastplate meet, And faith's broad shield before him spread.
3. With this omnipotence he moves; From this the alien armies flee; Till more than conqueror he proves, Through Christ, who gives him victory.
4. Thus strong in his Redeemer's strength, Sin, death, and hell he tramples down,—Fights the good fight; and takes at length, Through mercy, an immortal crown.

32 I Cannot Always Trace the Way. L. M.

Brackett.

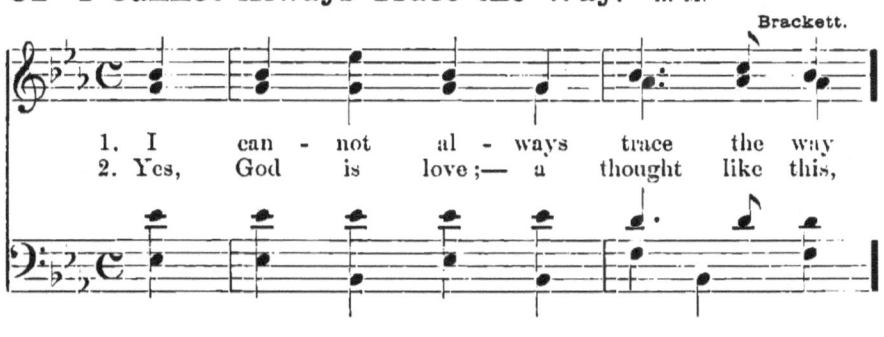

1. I cannot always trace the way
2. Yes, God is love;— a thought like this,

Where Thou, Almighty One, dost move; But I can always,
Can ev'ry gloomy thought remove, And turn all tears, all

ritard ad lib.

always say, That God is love, that God is love.
woes, to bliss. For God is love, for God is love.

CHRISTIAN SCIENCE HYMNAL.

33 Ward. L. M.

John Bowring.

Scotch Melody.
Arr. by Dr. Mason.

1. How sweet-ly flowed the gos-pel sound From lips of gen-tle-ness and grace, When list-'ning thou-sands gath-er'd round, And joy and rev-'rence filled the place!
2. From heav'n he came, of heav'n he spoke, To heav'n he led his fol-l'wers' way; Dark clouds of gloom-y night he broke, Un-veil-ing an im-mor-tal day.
3. "Come, wan-d'rers, to my Fa-ther's home; Come, all ye wea-ry ones, and rest:" Yes, sa-cred Teach-er, we will come, O-bey thee, love thee, and be blest.

34 O Love Divine, Whose Constant Beam. L. M.

John G. Whittier, abr. Barnby.

1. O Love Divine, whose constant beam Shines on the eyes that will not see, And waits to bless us while we dream, Thou leav'st us when we turn from Thee!

2. Nor bounds, nor clime, nor creed Thou know'st: Wide as our need, Thy favors fall The white wings of the Holy Ghost Stoop, unseen, o'er the heads of all.

35 Rockingham. L. M.

W. H. Drummond.
Lowell Mason.

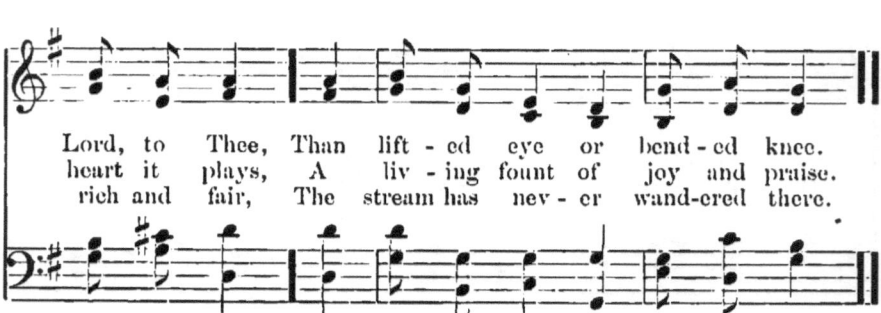

1. One cup of heal-ing oil and wine, One of-f'ring laid on mer-cy's shrine, Is thrice more grate-ful, Lord, to Thee, Than lift-ed eye or bend-ed knee.
2. In true and in-ward faith we trace The source of ev-'ry out-ward grace; With-in the pi-ous heart it plays, A liv-ing fount of joy and praise.
3. Kind deeds of peace and love be-tray Where'er the stream has found its way; But, where these spring not rich and fair, The stream has nev-er wand-ered there.

36 The Lifted Eye and Bended Knee. L. M.

Brackett.

1. The lifted eye, and bended knee,
Are but vain homage, Lord, to Thee;
In vain our lips Thy praise prolong,
The heart, a stranger to the song.

2. The pure, the humble, contrite mind,
Sincere, and to Thy will re-signed,
To Thee a nobler off'ring yields,
Than Sheba's groves, or Sharon's fields.

3. Love God and man— this great command,
Doth on eternal pillars stand;
This did Thine ancient prophets teach,
And this Thy Well-Belovèd preach.

The small notes are for accompaniment only.

37 Linwood. L.M.

Anon.
Givacchimo Rossini.

1. Be true and list the voice with-in, Be true un-to thy high i-deal, Thy per-fect self, that knows no sin— That self that is the on-ly real.
2. God is the on-ly per-fect One: My per-fect self, one must it be With God, then,—and that thought be-gun It solv-eth all the mys-ter-y.
3. If true to God, and God is Love, Then true to Love de-duce we then; "Be true" means, true to God a-bove, To self, and to our fel-low-men.

38 High in the Heavens, Eternal God.

I. Watts, alt. and abr.
G. M. Garrett.

1. High in the heav'ns, e-ter-nal God! Thy good-ness in full glo-ry shines; Thy truth shall break thro' ev-'ry cloud That vails and dark-ens Thy de-signs.
2. For-ev-er firm Thy jus-tice stands, As moun-tains their foun-da-tions keep: Wise are the won-ders of Thy hands; Thy judg-ments are a might-y deep.
3. Life, like a foun-tain rich and free, Springs from the pres-ence of my Lord; And in Thy light we all shall see The glo-ries prom-ised in thy word.

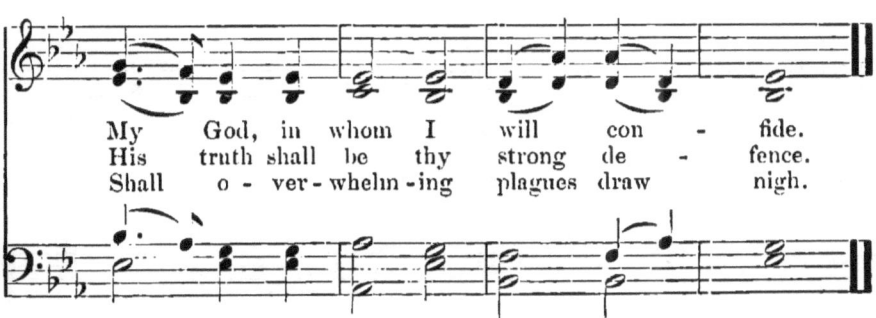

40 Press On, Dear Traveller, Press On. L. M. 6l.

Mrs. J. H. Bell.
William Henry Monk, Mus. Doc.

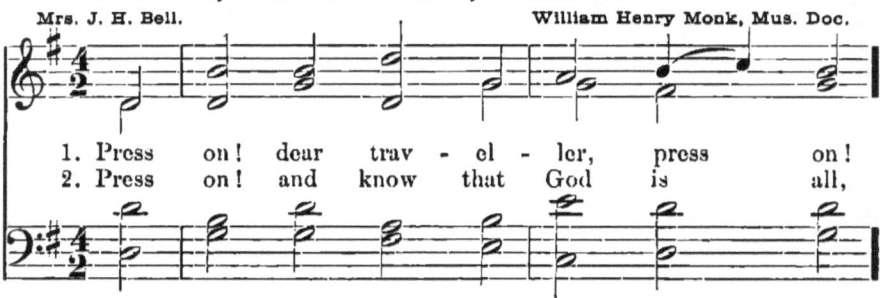

1. Press on! dear trav-el-ler, press on!
2. Press on! and know that God is all,

I am the Way, the Truth, the Life,
He is the Life, the Truth, the Love,

It is the straight and nar-row way
It is the way the Sav-iour trod,

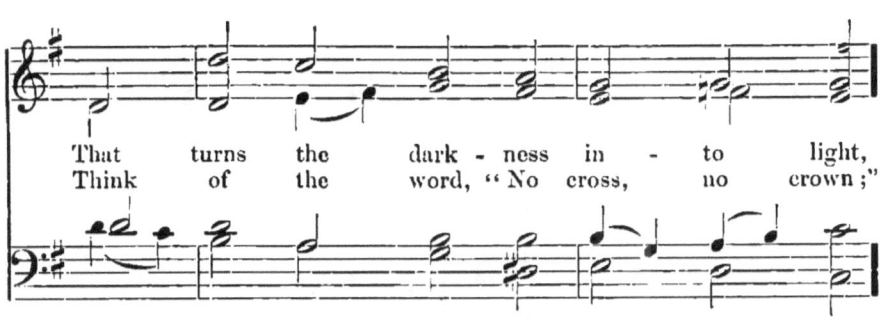

43 Dedham. C. M.

Wm. Gardiner.

1. Faith grasps the bless - ing she de - sires,
Hope points the up - ward gaze; And Love, ce - les - tial Love, in - spires The el - o - quence of praise.

2. But sweet - er far the still small voice,
Un - heard by hu - man ear, When God has made the heart re - joice, And dried the bit - er tear.

3. No ac - cents flow, no words as - cend;
All ut - ter-ance fail - eth there; But God Him - self doth com - pre - hend And an - swer si - lent prayer.

44 Happy the Heart Where Graces Reign. C. M.

Brackett.

1. Hap-py the heart where gra-ces reign,
2. Know-ledge— a - las! 'tis all in vain,
3. This is the grace that lives and sings,

Where love in-spires the breast: Love is the bright-est
And all in vain our fear; Our stub-born sins will
When faith and hope shall cease; 'Tis this shall strike our

of the train, And strength-ens all the rest.
fight and reign, If love be ab-sent there.
joy - ful strings, In bright-est realms of bliss.

45 Coronation. C. M.

F. W. Faber, alt.   Oliver Holden.

1. God's glo-ry is a wond'rous thing, Most strange in all its ways, And of all things on earth, least like What men a-gree to praise.
2. Oh, blest is he to whom is giv'n The in-stinct that can tell That God is on the field, when He Is most in-vis-i-ble!
3. And blest is he who can di-vine Where right doth real-ly lie, And dares to take the side that seems Wrong to man's blind-fold eye!
4. And right is right, since God is God; And right the day must win; To doubt would be dis-loy-al-ty, To fal-ter would be sin!

46 We Say to All Men Far and Near. C. M.

Novalis, abr. — Brackett.

1. We say to all men far and near
2. He lives; His presence hath not ceased,

That Christ has ris'n a-gain; That He is with us
Though foes and fears be rife; And thus we hail the

now and here, And ev-er shall re-main.
gos-pel feast, A world re-newed to life!

48 Oaksville. C. M.

C. Zeuner.

1. Scorn not the slight-est word or deed, Nor deem it void of pow'r; There's fruit in each wind-waft-ed seed, Wait-ing its na-tal hour.
2. No act falls fruit-less; none can tell How vast its pow'r may be; Nor what re-sults en-fold-ed dwell With-in it si-lent-ly.
3. Work and de-spair not; bring thy mite, Nor care how small it be; God is with all that serve the right, The ho-ly, true, and free.

50 Whatever Dims Thy Sense of Truth. C. M.

Brackett.

1. What-ev-er dims thy sense of truth, Or stains thy pur-i-ty, Though light as breath of sum-mer air, Count it as sin to thee.
2. Pre-serve the tab-let of thy thoughts From ev-'ry blem-ish free, While the Re-deem-er's low-ly faith Its tem-ple makes with thee.
3. And pray of God, that grace be giv'n To tread this nar-row way:— How dark so-ev-er it may seem, It leads to cloud-less day.

52 Oh! Ever on Our Earthly Path. C. M.

Sangster.

1. Oh! ev - er on our earth - ly path
2. Lift up the heart, lift up the mind!

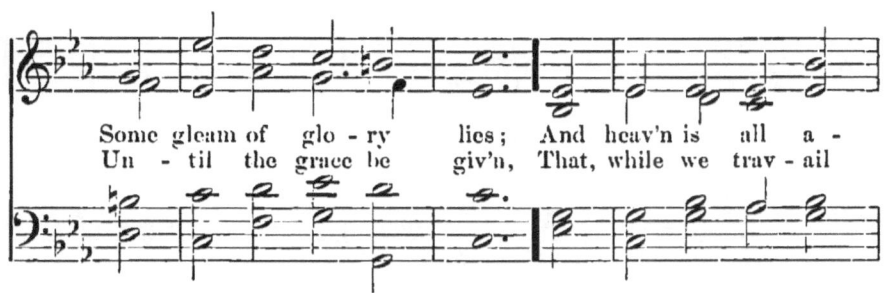

Some gleam of glo - ry lies; And heav'n is all a -
Un - til the grace be giv'n, That, while we trav - ail

round us now, If we but lift our eyes.
yet on earth, Our hearts may be in heav'n.

53 Naomi. C. M.

H. G. Naegeli.
Arr. by Lowell Mason.

1. Help us to help each other, Lord, Each other's cross to bear; Let each his friendly aid afford, And feel his brother's care.
2. Help us to build each other up, Our little stock improve; Increase our faith, confirm our hope, And perfect us in love.
3. Up into Thee, our living Head, Let us in all things grow; Till Thou hast made us free indeed, And spotless here below.

54 Church of the Ever-Living God. C. M.

H. Bonar, alt. and abr. J. V. Roberts, Mus. Doc.

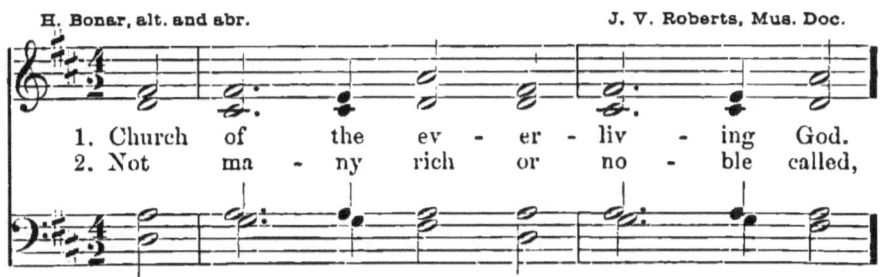

1. Church of the ev - er - liv - ing God.
2. Not ma - ny rich or no - ble called,

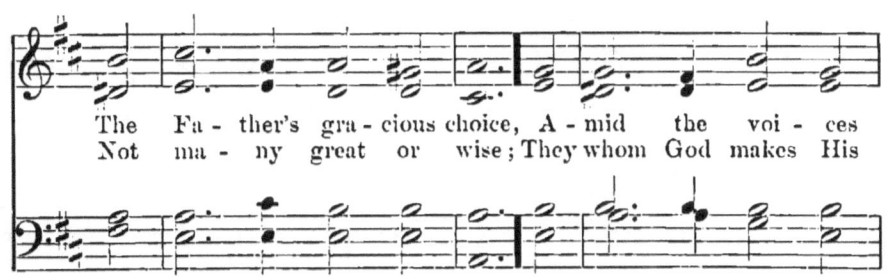

The Fa - ther's gra - cious choice, A - mid the voi - ces
Not ma - ny great or wise; They whom God makes His

of this earth How might - y is Thy voice!
kings and priests Are poor in hu - man eyes.

55 Maitland. C. M.
Milton, alt. and abr. — G. N. Allen.

1. How lovely are Thy dwellings, Lord, From noise and trouble free; How beautiful the sweet accord Of those who pray to Thee! . .
2. Lord God of Hosts, that reign'st on high, They are the truly blest Who on Thee only will rely, In Thee alone will rest. . .
3. For God the Lord, both sun and shield, Gives grace and glory bright; No good from him shall be withheld Whose ways are just and right. . .

56 Oh, Speed thee, Christian, on Thy Way. C. M.

1. Oh, speed thee, Christian, on thy way, And to thy ar-mor cling;... With gird-ed loins the call o-bey, That grace and mer-cy bring.
2. There is a bat-tle to be fought, An up-ward race to run;... A crown of glo-ry to be sought, A vic-t'ry to be won...
3. Oh, faint not, Christian! not with sighs Come thou be-fore His throne:... The race must come be-fore the prize, The cross be-fore the crown...

CHRISTIAN SCIENCE HYMNAL.

57 Balerma. C. M.

J. Swain. Hugh Wilson.

1. How sweet, how heav'n-ly is the sight, When those who love the Lord In one an-oth-er's peace de-light, And so ful-fill His word!
2. When, free from en-vy, scorn, and pride, Our wish-es all a-bove, Each can his broth-er's fail-ings hide, And show a broth-er's love!
3. Let love, in one de-light-ful stream, Through ev-'ry bos-om flow; And un-ion sweet, and dear es-teem In ev-'ry ac-tion glow.
4. Love is the gold-en chain that binds The hap-py hearts a-bove; And he's an heir of heav'n who finds His bos-om glow with love.

58 Beneath the Thick but Struggling Cloud. C. M.

Anon.   Vincent Novello.

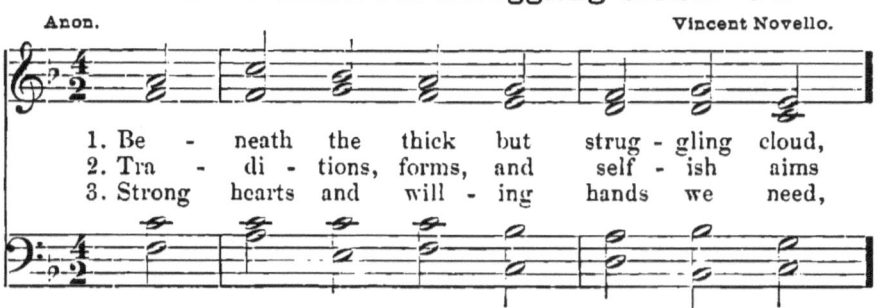

1. Beneath the thick but struggling cloud, We talk of Christian life; The words of Jesus on our lips, Our hearts with man at strife.
2. Traditions, forms, and selfish aims Have dimmed the inner light; Have closely veiled the spirit-world And angels from our sight.
3. Strong hearts and willing hands we need, Our temple to repair; Remove the gath'ring dust of years, And show the model fair.

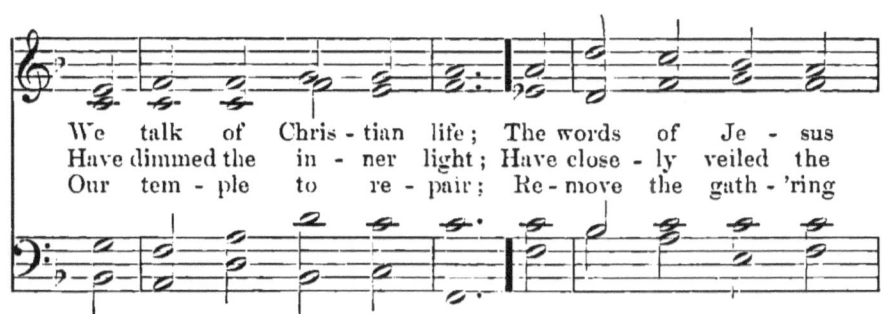

60 Speak Gently, it is Better Far. C. M.

Brackett.

1. Speak gent - ly, it is bet - ter far
2. Speak gent - ly to the err - ing: know
3. Speak gent - ly: 'tis a lit - tle thing,

To rule by love than fear; Speak gent - ly:
They must have toiled in vain; Per - chance un -
Dropped in the heart's deep well; The good, the

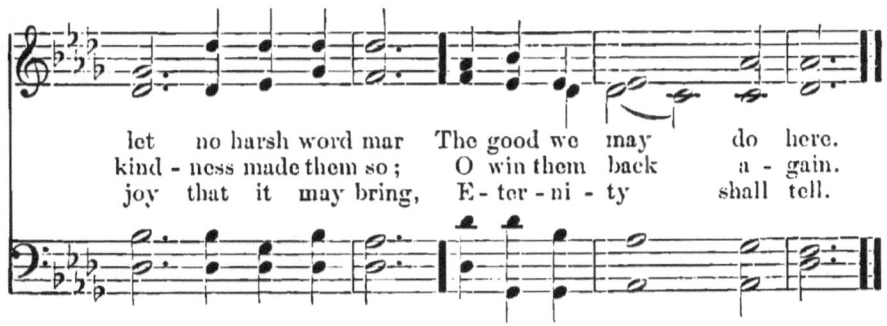

let no harsh word mar The good we may do here.
kind - ness made them so; O win them back a - gain.
joy that it may bring, E - ter - ni - ty shall tell.

62 Ye Timid Saints, Fresh Courage Take. C. M.

Cowper, alt, and abr. — Brackett.

1. Ye timid saints, fresh courage take! The clouds ye so much dread, Are big with mer-cy, and will break In bless-ings on your head.
2. His pur-pos-es will ri-pen fast, Un-fold-ing ev-'ry hour; The bud may have a bit-ter taste, But sweet will be the flow'r.
3. Blind un-be-lief is sure to err, And scan His work in vain; God is His own in-ter-pret-er, And He will make it plain.

67 Belmont. C. M.

W. H. Bathurst, abr.
Johann C. W. A. Mozart.

1. O for a faith that will not shrink, Though pressed by ev-'ry foe; That will not trem-ble on the brink Of a-ny earth-ly woe;
2. A faith that shines more bright and clear When tem-pests rage with-out; That when in dan-ger knows no fear, In dark-ness feels no doubt;
3. Oh, give us such a faith as this, And then, what-e'er may come, We'll taste, e'en here the hal-low'd bliss Of an e-ter-nal home.

69 Christmas. C. M.

John Morrison, abr. G. F. Handel.

1. To us a Child of Hope is born,
   To us a Son is giv'n;
   Him all the hosts of heav'n, Him all the hosts of heav'n.

2. His name shall be the Prince of Peace,
   For-ev-er-more a-dor'd;
   The great and might-y Lord! The great and might-y Lord!

3. His pow'r, in-creas-ing, still shall spread;
   His reign no end shall know;
   And peace a-bound be-low, And peace a-bound be-low.

Him shall the tribes of earth o-bey,
The Won-der-ful, the Counsel-lor,
Justice shall guard His throne above,

70 Lord! I Have Made Thy Words My Choice. C. M.

I. Watts, alt. and abr. — Brackett.

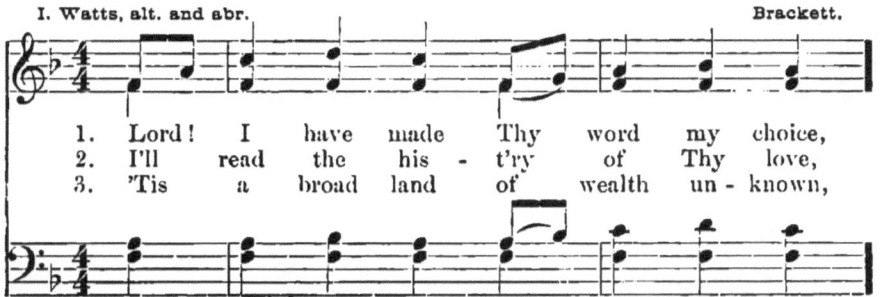

1. Lord! I have made Thy word my choice,
2. I'll read the his-t'ry of Thy love,
3. 'Tis a broad land of wealth un-known,

ALL VOICES in UNISON (or SOLO).

My last-ing her-i-tage: There shall my no-blest
And keep Thy law in sight, While thro' the prom-is-
Where springs of life a-rise; Seeds of im-mor-tal

pow'rs re-joice, My warm-est thoughts en-gage.
es I rove, With ev-er-fresh de-light.
bliss are sown, And hid-den glo-ry lies.

The small notes are for accompaniment only

71 Simpson. C. M.

John G. Whittier, abr.   From Louis Spohr

1. O Love! O Life! our faith and sight—
Thy presence maketh one: As, through transfigured clouds of white, We trace the noon-day sun.

2. We faintly hear, we dimly see,
In diff'ring phrase we pray; But, dim or clear, we own in Thee The Light, the Truth, the Way.

3. To do Thy will is more than praise,
As words are less than deeds; And simple trust can find Thy ways We miss with chart of creeds.

4. Our Friend, our Brother, and our Lord,
What may Thy service be? Nor name, nor form, nor ritual word, But simply foll'wing Thee.

72 We Walk by Faith of Joys to Come. C. M.

I. Watts, abr.   Brackett.

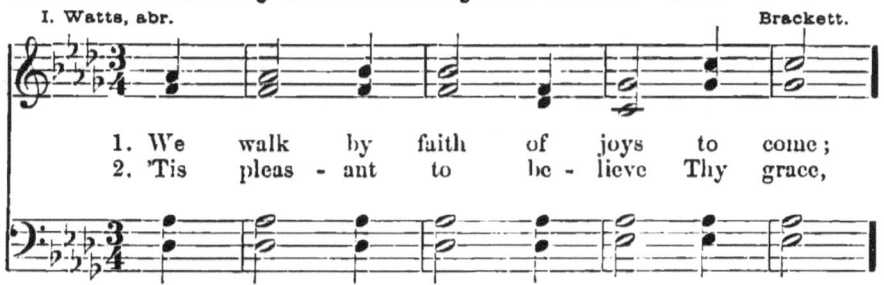

1. We walk by faith of joys to come;
2. 'Tis pleas-ant to be-lieve Thy grace,

Faith lives up-on His word; But while the bod-y
But we had rath-er see; We would be ab-sent

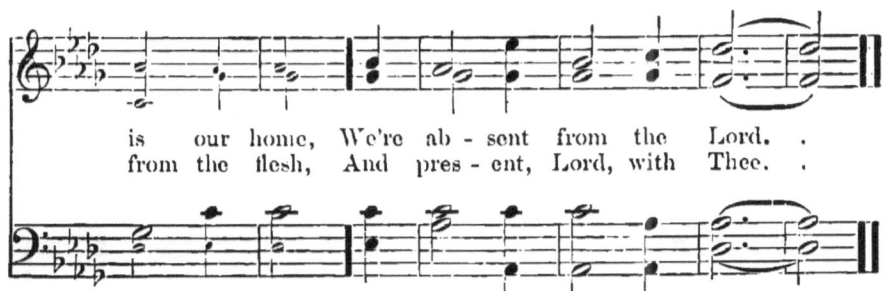

is our home, We're ab-sent from the Lord.
from the flesh, And pres-ent, Lord, with Thee.

The small notes are to be sung, but much softer than the large ones.

75 Heber. C. M.

Geo. W. Doane, alt.
Geo. Kingsley.

1. Thou art the Way: to Thee alone
From sin and death we flee;
And he who would the Father seek,
Must seek Him, Lord, by Thee.

2. Thou art the Truth: Thy word alone
True wisdom can impart;
Thou only canst unfold that Truth,
And purify the heart.

3. Thou art the Life: the rending tomb
Proclaims Thy conqu'ring arm;
And those who put their trust in Thee
Nor death nor hell shall harm.

4. Thou art the Way, the Truth, the Life,
Grant us that Way to know;
That Truth to keep, that Life to win,
Whose joys eternal flow.

76 Walk with Your God, Along the Road. C. M.

T. H. Gill.
Henry Smart.

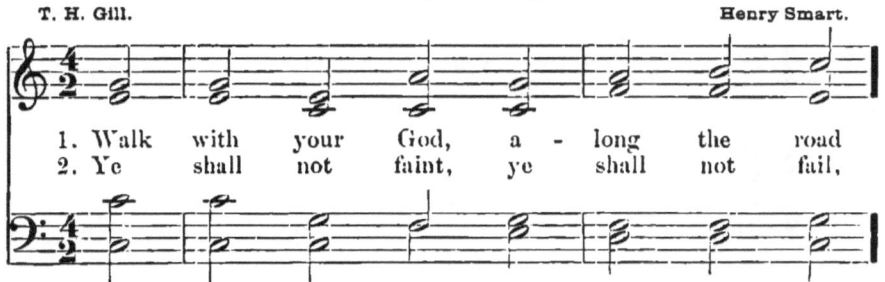

1. Walk with your God, along the road
2. Ye shall not faint, ye shall not fail,

Your strength He will renew; Wait on the ever-
Made in the spirit strong; Each task divine ye

lasting God, And He will work with you.
still shall hail, And blend it with a song.

78 I Cannot Walk in Darkness Long. C. M.

Caroline A. Mason, abr.   Rev. F. A. J. Hervey.

1. I cannot walk in darkness long.
2. He is my stay and my defence.

My Light is by my side: I cannot stumble
How shall I fail or fall? My keeper is Om-

or go wrong, While fol-l'wing such a guide.
ni-po-tence; My Ruler rul-eth all.

81 Southport. C. M.

George Kingsley.

1. In atmosphere of love divine,
We live, and move, and breathe;
Tho' mortal eyes may see it not;
'Tis sense that would deceive.

2. The Principal of being, God,
Is with us ev'ry-where;
He holds us perfect in His love,
And we His image bear.

3. The mortal sense we must destroy,
If we would bring to light
The wonders of eternal Mind,
Where sense is lost in sight.

82 The Loving Friend to All Who Bowed. C. M.

Samuel Longfellow.   Isaac Smith.

1. The loving friend to all who bowed
Beneath life's weary load, From lips baptized in humble pray'r, His consolations flowed.

2. The faithful witness to the truth,
His just rebuke was hurled Out from a heart that burned to break The fetters of the world.

3. No hollow rite, no lifeless creed,
His piercing glance could bear; But longing hearts which sought Him found That God and heav'n were there.

84. Beneath the Shadow of the Cross. C. M.

Samuel Longfellow. — Brackett.

1. Beneath the shadow of the cross,
As earthly hopes remove,
His new commandment Jesus gives,—
His blessed word of love.

2. O bond of union, strong and deep!
O bond of perfect peace!
Not e'en the lifted cross can harm,
If we but hold to this.

3. Then, Jesus, be thy Spirit ours;
And swift our feet shall move
To deeds of pure self-sacrifice,
And the sweet tasks of love.

85 St. Martin's. C. M.

Samuel Longfellow, abr. — Wm. Tansur.

1. One holy Church of God appears
Thro' ev-'ry age and race, Un-wast-ed
by the lapse of years, Un-changed by chang-ing place.

2. From old-est time, on far-thest shores,
Be-neath the pine or palm, One Un-seen
Pres-ence she a-dores, With si-lence or with psalm.

3. Her priests are all God's faith-ful sons,
To serve the world raised up; The pure in
heart her bap-tized ones; Love, her com-mu-nion-cup.

87 Eckhardtsheim. C. M.

C. Zeuner.

1. Lowly in heart to all who sought, A friend and servant found; He washed their feet, he wiped their tears, And healed each bleeding wound.
2. Midst keen reproach and cruel scorn, Patient and meek he stood; His foes, ungrateful, sought his life; He labored for their good.
3. Jesus our pattern and our guide, His cross may we all bear, O may we tread his holy steps, His joy and glory share.

89 St. Asaph. C. M. D.

J. M. Giornovichi.

1. It came upon the midnight clear, That glorious song of old, . . The angels bending near the earth Their wondrous story told;
2. O ye, beneath life's crushing load, Whose forms are bending low, . . Who toil along the climbing way With painful steps and slow!
3. For lo, the days are hast'ning on, By prophets seen of old, . . When with the ever-circling years Shall come the time foretold,

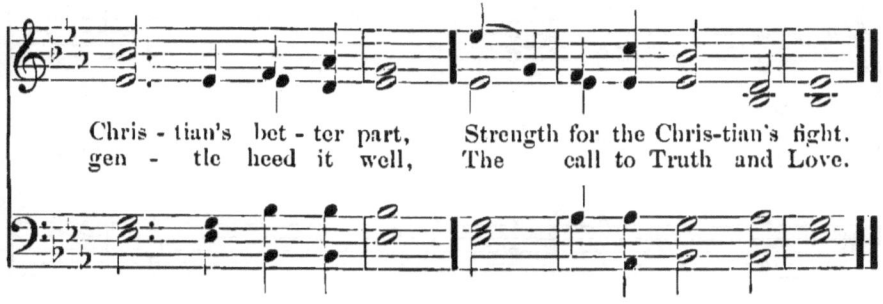

92 Eternal Mind the Potter Is. C. M. D.

Alice Dayton.   Louis Sphor.

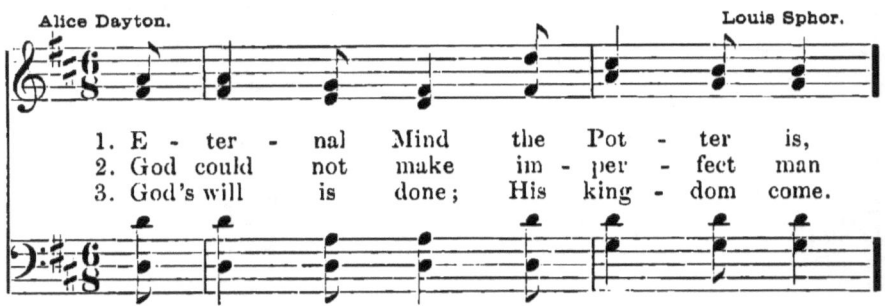

1. E-ter-nal Mind the Pot-ter is,
2. God could not make im-per-fect man
3. God's will is done; His king-dom come.

And thought, th' e-ter-nal clay. The hand that fash-ion
His mod-el In-fi-nite; Un-hal-lowed thought He
The Pot-ter's work is plain. The long-ing to be

is di-vine; His works pass not a-way...
could not plan—Love's work and Love must fit...
good and true Has brought the Light a-gain;

94 Our Heaven is Everywhere. S. M.

Miss Fletcher, alt. and abr. — Brackett.

1. Our heav'n is ev - 'ry - where,
   If we but love our God, . . Un-swerv-ing tread the nar - row way, And ev - er shun the broad.
2. 'Tis where the trust - ing heart
   Bows meek - ly to its grief, . . Still look - ing up with ear - nest faith For com - fort and re - lief.
3. Wher - ev - er truth a - bides,
   Sweet peace is ev - er there; . . If we but love and serve the Lord, Our heav'n is ev - 'ry - where.

CHRISTIAN SCIENCE HYMNAL.

95 Thatcher. S. M.

Anon.
George Frederick Handel.

1. O Spirit, source of light, Thy grace is unconfined; Dispel the gloomy shades of night, Reveal the light of Mind.
2. Now to our eyes display The truth Thy words reveal; Cause us to run the heav'nly way, Delighting in Thy will.
3. Thy teachings make us know The mys't'ries of Thy love, The vanity of things below, The joy of things above.

96 Imposture Shrinks from Light. S. M.

Scott, alt. and abr.
Brackett.

1. Im - pos - ture shrinks from light, . . And dreads the piercing eye; . . But sa - cred truths the test in - vite, They bid us search and try. . .
2. With un - der - stand - ing blest, . . Cre - at - ed to be free, . . Our faith on man we dare not rest, Sub - ject to none but Thee. .
3. The truth Thou dost im - part, . . May we with firm - ness own; . . Ab - horr - ing each e - va - sive art, And fear - ing Thee a - lone. . .

97 State Street. S. M.

Alt. and abr.
Jonathan C. Woodman.

1. Come to the land of peace; From shad-ows come a-way; Where all the sounds of weep-ing cease, And storms no more have sway.
2. Fear hath no dwell-ing here; But pure re-pose and love Breathe through the bright, ce-les-tial air The spir-it of the dove.
3. In this di-vine a-bode Change leaves no sad-d'ning trace; Come, trust-ing heart, come weep-ing to thy God, Thy ho-ly rest-ing-place.

Used by permission of Oliver Ditson Company, owners of the copyright.

98 Let Party Names No More. S. M.

B. Beddome.   Brackett.

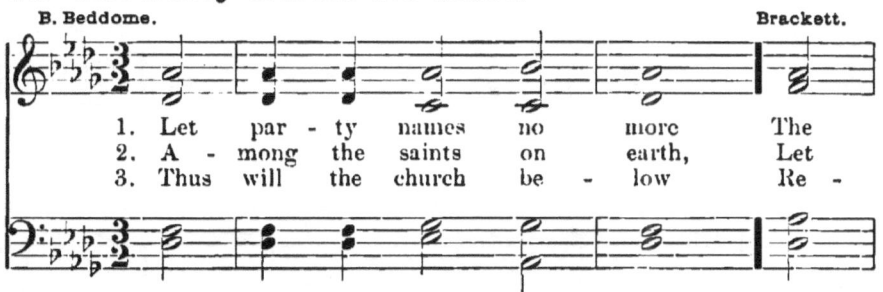

1. Let party names no more
The Christian world o'er-spread;
Gentile and Jew, and bond and free,
Are one in Christ their head.

2. Among the saints on earth,
Let mutual love be found;
Heirs of the same inheritance,
With mutual blessings crowned.

3. Thus will the church below
Resemble that above;
Where streams of pleasure ever flow,
And ev-'ry heart is love.

99 Laban. S. M.

M. J. H. Zink, abr.   Lowell Mason.

1. Thine is a living way; In death it has no part; From fear of all disease and sin, It will relieve the heart.
2. Oh blessed, blessed Light! Oh joyful, joyful news! Thy law is Life, Thy way is peace, No other can we choose.
3. The Spirit's sweet control Freely we will confess,—. Fly to Thine out-stretched arms of love, And there find health and rest.

100 Teach Me, My God and King. S. M.

Rev. Geo. Herbert, abr.   Brackett.

1. Teach me, my God and King, In all things Thee to see; And what I do in a-ny thing, To do it as for Thee.
2. To scorn the sens-es' sway While still to Thee I tend; In all I do be Thou the way,— In all be Thou the end.
3. If done beneath Thy laws, E'en servile labors shine; Hallow'd is toil, if this the cause, The meanest work divine.

The small notes are for accompaniment only.

102 Servants of Christ, Arise. S. M.

Mrs. Lydia H. Sigourney, abr. — Brackett.

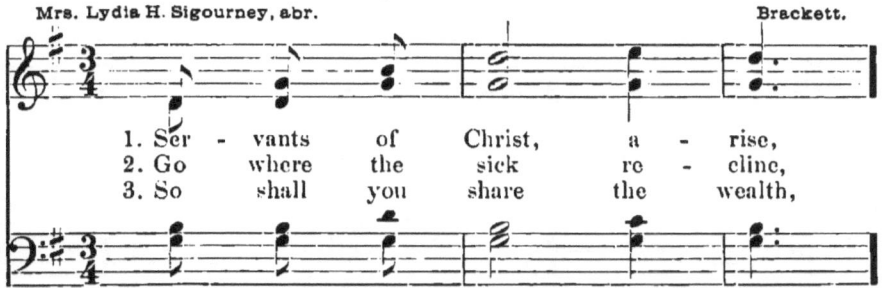

1. Servants of Christ, arise, And gird you for the toil. The dew of promise from the skies Already cheers the soil.
2. Go where the sick recline, Where mourning hearts deplore; And where the sons of sorrow pine, Dispense your hallow'd lore.
3. So shall you share the wealth, That earth may ne'er despoil, And the blest gospel's saving health Repay your arduous toil.

The small notes are for accompaniment only.

103 Boylston. S. M.
C. Wesley, abr. — Lowell Mason.

1. Soldiers of Christ, arise, And put your armor on, Strong is the strength which God supplies Through His eternal Son.
2. Stand then in His great might, With all His strength endued, And take, to arm you for the fight, The panoply of God.
3. From strength to strength go on; Wrestle, and fight, and pray; Tread all the pow'rs of darkness down, And win the well-fought day.

105 Athol. S. M.

Doddridge. — Ralph Harrison.

1. Ye servants of the Lord! Each in his office wait, Observant of His heav'nly word, And watchful at His gate.
2. Let all your lamps be bright, And trim the golden flame; Gird up your loins as in His sight, For perfect is His name.
3. Watch,—'tis your Lord's command; And while we speak He's near; Mark the first signal of His hand, And ready all appear.
4. Oh, happy servant he, In such a posture found! He shall his Lord with rapture see, And be with honor crowned.

108 Sow in the Morn Thy Seed. S. M.

J. Montgomery.   Brackett.

1. Sow in the morn thy seed, At
2. And du-ly shall ap-pear In

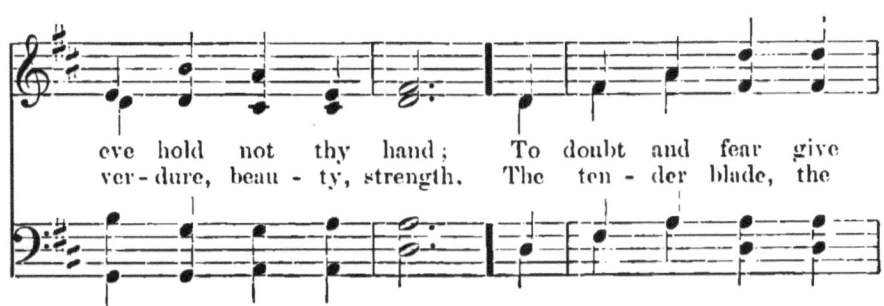

eve hold not thy hand; To doubt and fear give
ver-dure, beau-ty, strength. The ten-der blade, the

thou no heed; Broad-cast it o'er the land.
stalk, the ear, And the full corn at length.

110 Make Haste, O Man to Do. S. M.

H. Bonar, alt. and abr.
Brackett.

1. Make haste, O man, to do What ever must be done; Thou hast no time to lose in sloth, When all to Truth must come.
2. Up then, with speed and work; Fling ease and self away— This is no time for thee to sleep — Up, watch, and work, and pray!

112 Call the Lord Thy Sure Salvation 8s, 7s.

James Montgomery, abr.
Rev. J. B. Dykes, Mus. Doc.

1. Call the Lord thy sure sal - va - tion, Rest be - neath th'Al - might - y's shade; In His se - cret hab - i - ta - tion Dwell, nor ev - er be dis-mayed.
2. He shall charge His an - gel le - gions Watch and ward o'er thee to keep, Though thou walk thro' hos - tile re - gions, Though in des - ert wilds thou sleep.
3. There no tu - mult can a - larm thee, Thou shalt dread no hid - den snare; Guile nor vi - o - lence shall harm thee In e - ter - nal safe - guard there.

113 Bartimeus. 8s, 7s.

S. Johnson, abr. Stephen Jenks.

1. Onward, Christian, though the region
Where thou art be drear and lone;
God hath set a guardian legion
Very near thee,— press thou on!

2. By the thorn-road, and none other,
Is the mount of vision won;
Tread it without shrinking, brother!
Jesus trod it,— press thou on!

3. By thy trustful, calm endeavor,
Guiding, cheering, like the sun,
Earth-bound hearts thou shalt deliver;
Oh, for their sake,— press thou on!

115 Rathbun. 8s, 7s.

Gottfried Arnold. Tr. by Miss C. Winkworth, alt. and abr. I. Conkey.

1. Well for him who all things los-ing, E'en him-self doth count as naught, Still the one thing need-ful choos-ing, That with all true bliss is fraught!
2. Well for him who noth-ing know-eth But his God, whose bound-less love Makes the heart where-in it glow-eth Calm and pure and faith-ful prove!
3. Well for him who all for-sak-ing, Walk-eth not in shad-ows vain, But the path of peace is tak-ing Through this vale of tears and pain!
4. O that we our hearts might sev-er From earth's tempt-ing van-i-ties, Fix-ing them on Him for-ev-er In whom all our full-ness lies!

116 Cast Thy Bread upon the Waters. 8s, 7s.

J. H. Hansford, alt. and abr.
Brackett.

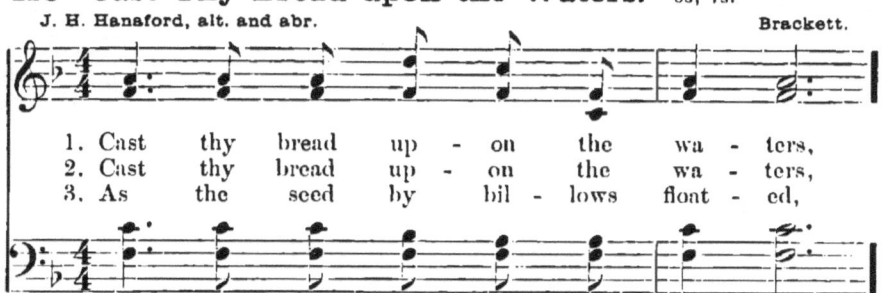

1. Cast thy bread up-on the wa-ters,
2. Cast thy bread up-on the wa-ters,
3. As the seed by bil-lows float-ed,

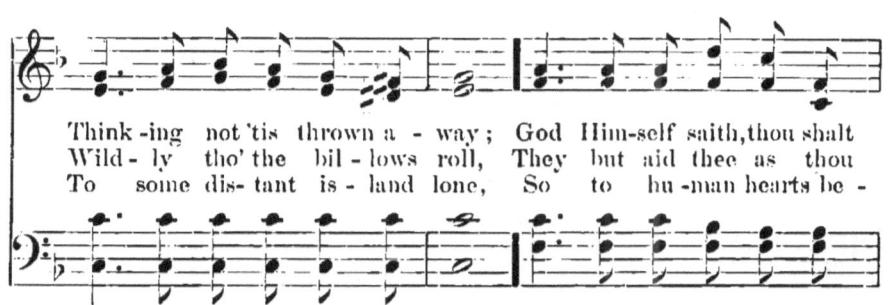

Think-ing not 'tis thrown a-way; God Him-self saith, thou shalt
Wild-ly tho' the bil-lows roll, They but aid thee as thou
To some dis-tant is-land lone, So to hu-man hearts be-

gath - er   It   a - gain some fu - ture day.
toil - est   Truth to spread from pole to pole.
night - ed, That thou fling - est may be borne.

117 Stockwell. 8s, 7s.

D. E. Jones.

1. Hear our pray'r, oh gracious Father, Author of celestial good, That Thy laws so pure and holy May be better understood.
2. Armed with faith may we press onward, Knowing nothing but Thy will, Conqu'ring ev'ry storm of error, With the sweet words, "Peace be still."
3. Like the star of Beth-l'hem shining, Love will guide us all the way, From the depths of error's darkness, Into Truth's eternal day.

118 Know, O Child, Thy Full Salvation. 8s, 7s.

Henry Francis Lyte, alt. and abr.　　　John Sebastian Bach. Arr. by Steggall.

1. Know, O child, thy full salvation; Rise o'er sin and fear and care; Joy to find, in ev - 'ry sta - tion, Some-thing still to do, or bear.
2. Think what spir - it dwells with - in thee; Think what Fa - ther's smiles are thine; Think what Je - sus did to win thee; Child of heav'n, can'st thou re - pine?
3. Haste thee on from grace to glo - ry, Arm'd with faith and wing'd with pray'r, Heav'n's e - ter - nal day be - fore thee, God's own hand shall guide thee there.

120 Father, Hear the Prayer We Offer. 8s. 7s.

Hymns of the Spirit, abr.   Brackett.

1. Father, hear the pray'r we offer: Not for ease that pray'r shall be; But for strength, that we may ever Live our lives courageously.
2. Not for ever in green pastures Do we ask our way to be; But the steep and rugged pathway May we tread rejoicingly.
3. Not for ever by still waters Would we idly quiet stay; But would smite the living fountains From the rocks along our way.

121 Science. 8s, 7s.

Laura C. Nourse, alt. and abr.
Brackett.

1. Now sweeping down the years untold,
   The day of Truth is breaking; And sweet and fair the
   leaves unfold, Of Love's immortal waking.

2. For flow'r and fruitage now are seen,
   Where blight and mildew rested: The Christ to-day to
   us, has been By word and deed attested.

3. His living presence we have felt—
   The "word made flesh" among us: And hearts of stone before Him melt—
   His peace is brooding o'er us.

122. With Love and Peace and Joy Supreme. 8s, 7s.

Laura C. Nourse, alt. and abr.
Rev. J. B. Dykes, Mus. Doc.

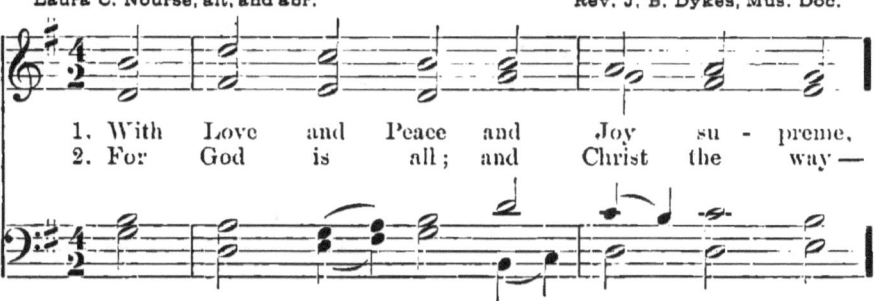

1. With Love and Peace and Joy supreme, We hail the new appearing; From out the darkness and the dream, The hav'n of rest is nearing.
2. For God is all; and Christ the way— Earth's meek and bold defender— Has cleft the night, and lo! the day Bursts forth in mighty splendor.

124 Vainly Through Night's Weary Hours. 8s, 7s.

H. Auber, abr.   Brackett.

1. Vain - ly, through night's wea - ry hours,
Keep we watch, lest foes a-larm; Vain our bul - warks, and our tow - ers, But for God's pro - tect - ing arm.

2. Vain were all our toil and la - bor,
Did not God that la - bor bless; Vain, with-out His grace and fa - vor, Ev - 'ry tal - ent we pos - sess.

3. Vain - er still the hope of heav - en,
That on hu - man strength relies; But to him shall help be giv - en, Who in hum - ble faith ap - plies.

125 Autumn. 8s, 7s, D.

Mrs. F. S. Lovejoy.   Spanish Melody. Marechio.

1. O, my people! jour-n'ying on-ward,—
You of Christ's great brother-hood, Heed the les-sons which He
gives you, Writ-ten in His bless-ed word.

2. This the path which you must fol-low,
This the way the Sav-iour trod; And He teach-es this will
lead you In - to peace and up to God.

3. If you will but heed this les-son,
Which the bless-ed Sav-iour gave, Go-ing out in - to the
by - ways Seek-ing those He came to save,

CHRISTIAN SCIENCE HYMNAL.

Strong and clear and full of mean-ing:
'Tis in deeds we serve the Mas-ter,—
Tell-ing them the won-drous sto-ry,

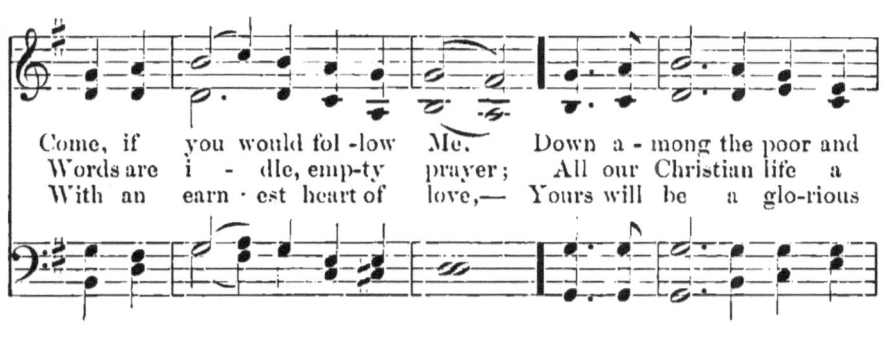

Come, if you would fol-low Me. Down a-mong the poor and
Words are i-dle, emp-ty prayer; All our Christian life a
With an earn-est heart of love,— Yours will be a glo-rious

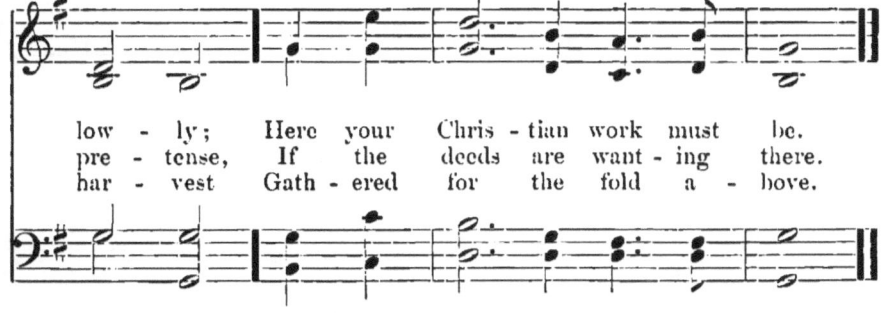

low-ly; Here your Chris-tian work must be.
pre-tense, If the deeds are want-ing there.
har-vest Gath-ered for the fold a-bove.

126 True, the Heart Grows Rich in Giving. 8s, 7s, D.

Elizabeth Charles, alt. and abr.   F. J. Haydn.

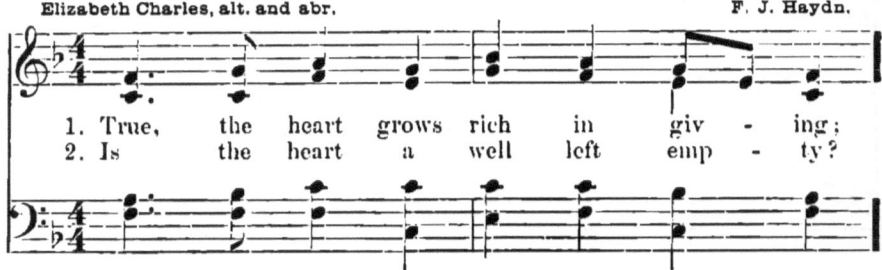

1. True, the heart grows rich in giv - ing;
2. Is the heart a well left emp - ty?

All its wealth is liv - ing grain; Seeds which mil - dew
None but God its void can fill; Noth - ing but a

in the gar - ner, Scat - tered, fill with gold the plain.
cease-less Foun-tain Can its cease - less long - ings still.

127 Bavaria. 8s, 7s, D.

F. L. Heywood, alt. and abr.
German.

1. Break-ing through the clouds of dark-ness,
2. Christ-like in its ben-e-dic-tions,

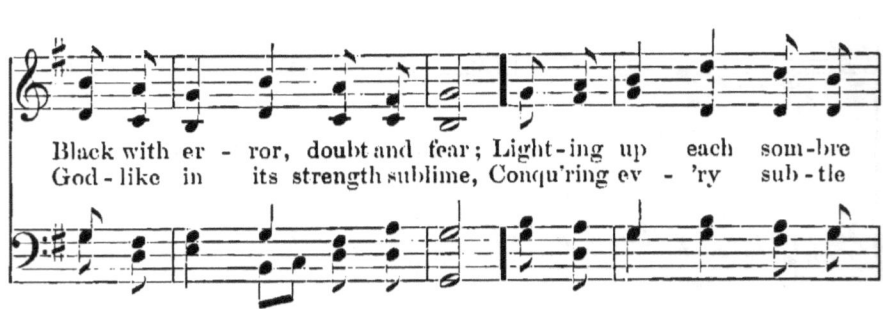

Black with er-ror, doubt and fear; Light-ing up each som-bre
God-like in its strength sublime, Conqu'ring ev-'ry sub-tle

shad-ow, With a ra-diance soft and clear;
er-ror, With a meek-ness all di-vine,—

128 Peace be to this Congregation. 8s, 7s, D.

Wesleyan.   Brackett.

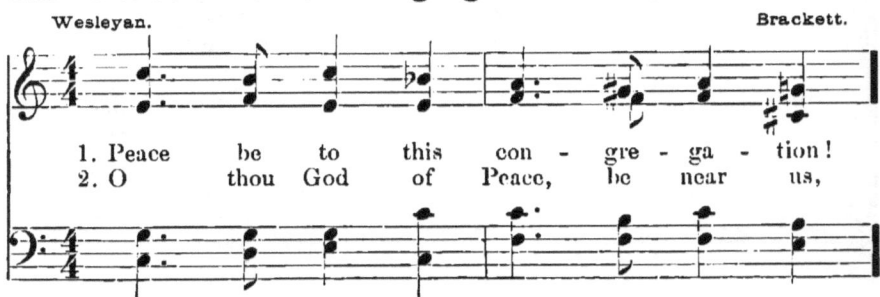

1. Peace be to this con - gre - ga - tion!
2. O thou God of Peace, be near us,

Peace to ev - 'ry heart there - in! Peace, the ear - nest
Fix with - in our hearts Thy home; With Thy bright ap -

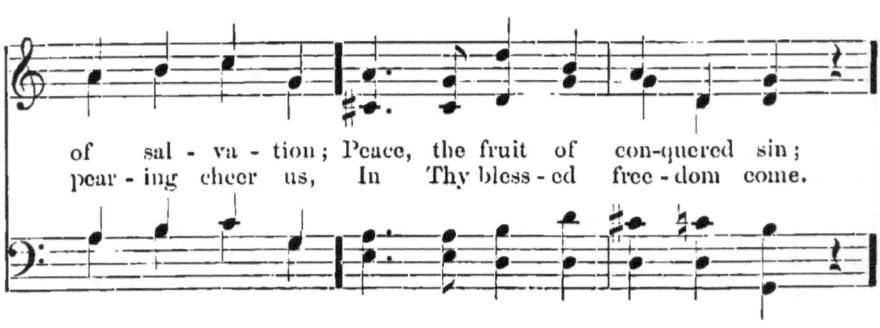

of sal - va - tion; Peace, the fruit of con - quered sin;
pear - ing cheer us, In Thy bless - ed free - dom come.

129 Greenville. 8s, 7s, D.

Anon, alt.   Rosseau.

1. Ho - ly Fa - ther, Thou hast taught us
2. We would trust in Thy pro - tect - ing,

We should live to Thee a - lone; Year by year, Thy
Whol - ly rest up - on Thine arm, Fol - low whol - ly

hand hath brought us, On through dan-gers oft un - known,
Thy di - rect - ing, Thou our on - ly guard from harm!

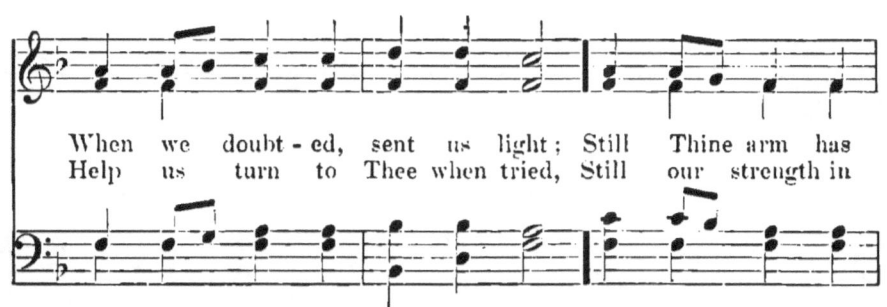

130 He That Goeth Forth with Weeping. 8s, 7s, D.

Hastings, alt.   Charles Harford Lloyd, Mus. Bac.

1. He that go-eth forth with weep-ing,
2. Sow thy seed, be nev-er wea-ry

Bear-ing still the prec-ious seed, Nev-er
Let not fear thy thoughts em - ploy; Though the

tir - ing, nev-er sleep-ing, Soon shall see his toil suc - ceed:
pros-pect be most drear - y, Thou may'st reap the fruits of joy:

CHRISTIAN SCIENCE HYMNAL.

Show'rs of rain will fall from heav-en,
Lo! the scene of ver-dure bright-'ning

Then the cheer-ing sun will shine, So shall
See the ris-ing grain ap-pear; Look a-

plen-teous fruit be giv-en, Through an in-fluence all di-vine.
gain! the fields are whit-'ning, Har-vest-time is sure-ly near.

131 Weimar. 8s, 7s, 4s.

Kelly, alt. Ancient Melody, 1648.

1. Look, ye saints! the day is breaking; Joyful times are near at hand; God, the mighty God, is speaking By His word in ev'ry land: Day advances—Darkness flees at His command.

2. God of Jacob, high and glorious! Let Thy people see Thy pow'r; Let the gospel be victorious Thro' the world for evermore: Then shall idols Perish, while Thy saints adore.

132 Every Human Tie May Perish. 8s, 7s, 4s.

Rev. Thomas Kelly, abr. Brackett.

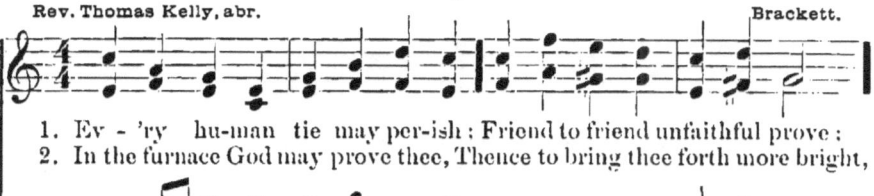

1. Ev - 'ry hu-man tie may per-ish: Friend to friend unfaithful prove;
2. In the furnace God may prove thee, Thence to bring thee forth more bright,

Mothers cease their own to cher-ish; Heav'n and earth at last re-move:
But can nev - er cease to love thee; Thou art prec-ious in His sight:

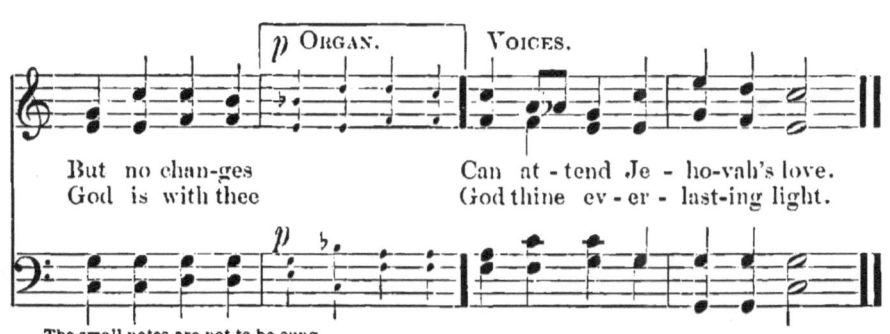

But no chan-ges   Can at-tend Je - ho-vah's love.
God is with thee   God thine ev - er - last-ing light.

The small notes are not to be sung.

133 Zion. 8s, 7s, 4s.

Anon. — Thomas Hastings.

1. Come, Thou all-transforming Spirit,
2. Oh, may all enjoy the blessing

Bless the sower and the seed;
Which Thy word's designed to give;

Let each heart Thy grace inherit;
Let us all, Thy love possessing,—

134 Guide me, O Thou Great Jehovah! 8s, 7s, 4s.

William Williams, alt. and abr. — Brackett.

1. Guide me, O Thou great Jehovah!
3. Open is the crystal fountain,

Pilgrim through this barren land:
Whence the healing waters flow:

I am weak, but Thou art mighty,
And the fiery cloudy pillar

Hold me with Thy pow'r-ful hand.
Leads me all my jour-ney through.

Bread of heav - en!
Strong De - liv - 'rer!

Feed me till I want no more.
Still Thou art my strength and shield.

135 Nuremburg. 7s.

Josiah Conder.
Johann Rudolph Ahle.

1. Day by day the man-na fell: Oh, to learn this les-son well! Still by con-stant mer - cy fed, Give me, Lord, my dai - ly bread.
2. Day by day the prom - ise reads, "Dai-ly strength for dai - ly needs: Cast fore - bod-ing fears a - way; Take the man - na of to - day."
3. Lord, my times are in Thy hand: All my san-guine hopes have planned, To Thy wis-dom I re - sign, And would mould my will to Thine.
4. Thou my dai - ly task shalt give; Day by day to Thee I live; So shall add - ed years ful - fil Not my own, my Fa - ther's will.

136 Everlasting Arms of Love. 7s.

Anon.   Brackett.

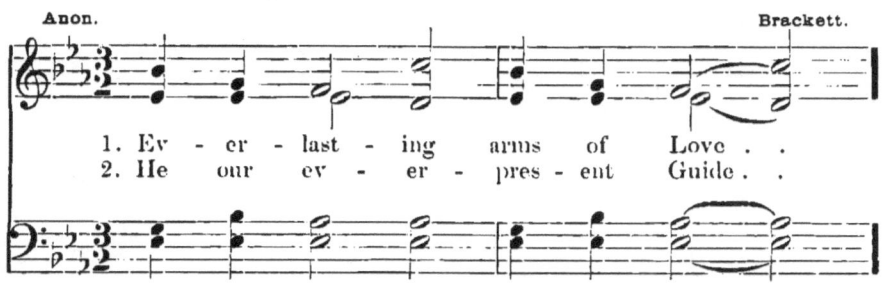

1. Ev - er - last - ing arms of Love
2. He our ev - er - pres - ent Guide

Are be-neath, a-round, a-bove; God it is who
Faith-ful is what-e'er be-tide; Glad-ly, then, we

bears us on, . . His the arm we lean up - on.
jour - ney on, . . With His arm to lean up - on.

137 Hendon. 7s.

William Gaskell, abr. and alt.
C. H. A. Malan.

1. Might-y God, the First, the Last, What are a-ges in Thy sight But as yes-ter-day when past, Or a watch with-in the night? Or a watch with-in the night?
2. All that be-ing e'er shall know, On, still on, thro' far-thest years, All e-ter-ni-ty can show, Bright be-fore Thee now ap-pears, Bright be-fore Thee now ap-pears.
3. What so-e'er our lot may be, Calm-ly in this tho't we'll rest,—When we see as Thou dost see, We shall love Thee and be blest, We shall love Thee and be blest.

138 Partners of a Glorious Hope. 7s.

1. Part-ners of a glo-rious hope! Lift your hearts and voi-ces up; No-bly let us bear the strife, Keep the ho-li-ness of life;
2. Still for-get the things be-hind, Fol-low God the on-ly Mind, To the mark un-wea-ried press, Seize the crown of right-eous-ness.
3. In our lives our faith be known, Faith by ho-ly ac-tions shown; Faith that moun-tains can re-move, Faith that al-ways works by love.

The small notes are for accompaniment only.

141 Dijon. 7s.

Anon.
German Evening Hymn.

1. They who seek the throne of grace,
2. In our sick-ness, in our health;
3. Then, my heart, in ev-'ry strait,

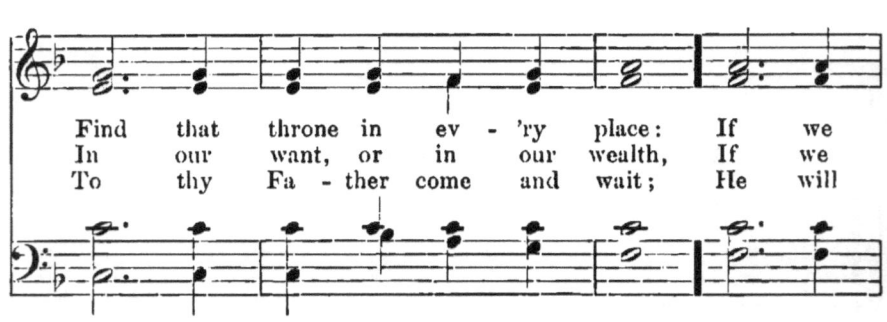

Find that throne in ev-'ry place: If we
In our want, or in our wealth, If we
To thy Fa-ther come and wait; He will

live a life of pray'r, God is pres-ent ev-'ry-where.
look to God in pray'r, God is pres-ent ev-'ry-where.
an-swer ev-'ry pray'r, God is pres-ent ev-'ry-where.

142 Holy Bible! Book Divine! 7s.

Anon, abr.   Brackett.

1. Holy Bible! book divine!
Precious treasure! thou art mine:
Mine to tell me whence I came;
Mine to tell me what I am;—

2. Mine to chide me when I rove,
Mine to show a Saviour's love;
Mine thou art to guide and guard;
Mine to give a rich reward;—

3. Mine to comfort in distress,
If the Holy Spirit bless:
Mine to show, by living faith,
Man can triumph over death.

143 Herford. 7s.

Lowell. — English Tune.

1. They are slaves who will not choose Hatred, scoffing, and abuse, Rather than, in silence, shrink From the truth they needs must think.
2. They are slaves who fear to speak For the fallen and the weak; They are slaves, who dare not be In the right with two or three.

144 God Made All His Creatures Free. 7s.

Montgomery, alt. and abr.
Myles B. Foster.

1. God made all His crea-tures free;
2. So shall all our slav-ery cease,

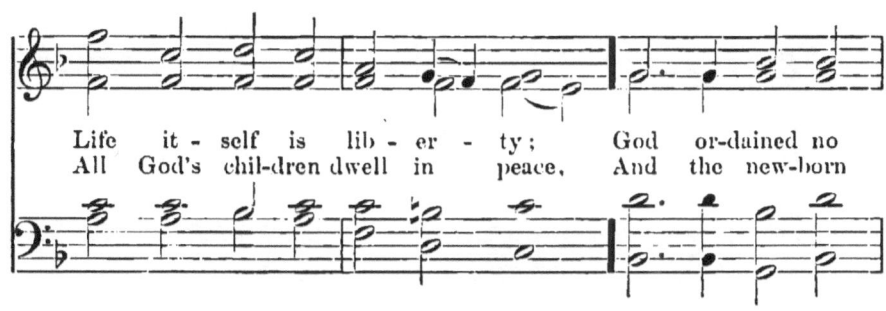

Life it-self is lib-er-ty; God or-dained no
All God's chil-dren dwell in peace, And the new-born

oth-er bands Than u-nit-ed hearts and hands.
earth re-cord Love, and Love a-lone, is Lord.

145 Halle. 7s, 6l.

Thomas Toke Lynch, 1855, abr. F. J. Haydn.

1. Gracious spirit, dwell with me;
2. Truthful spirit, dwell with me;
3. Mighty spirit, dwell with me;

I myself would gracious be,
I myself would truthful be,
I myself would mighty be,

And, with words that help and heal,
And with wisdom kind and clear
Mighty so as to prevail

CHRISTIAN SCIENCE HYMNAL.

Would Thy life in mine re - veal;
Let Thy life in mine ap - pear;
Where un - aid - ed man must fail;

And with ac - tions bold and meek
And with ac - tions broth - er - ly
Ev - er by a might - y hope

Christ's own gra - cious spir - it speak.
Fol - low Christ's sin - cer - i - ty.
Press - ing on and bear - ing up.

CHRISTIAN SCIENCE HYMNAL.

147 Webb. 7s, 6s, D.

S. F. Smith.   G. J. Webb.

1. The morn - ing light is break - ing;
2. Blest riv - er of sal - va - tion!

The dark - ness dis - ap - pears! The sons of earth are
Pur - sue thine on - ward way; Flow thou to ev - 'ry

wak - ing To pen - i - ten - tial tears;
na - tion, Nor in thy rich - ness stay:

148 God Comes with Succor Speedy. 7s, 6s, D.

James Montgomery, abr. Brackett.

1. God comes, with succor speedy,
2. To Him shall pray'r unceasing,

To those who suffer wrong; To help the poor and
And daily vows, ascend; His kingdom still in-

needy, And bid the weak be strong;
creasing, A kingdom without end.

CHRISTIAN SCIENCE HYMNAL.

He comes to break op - pres - sion,
The tide of time shall nev - - er

And set the cap - tive free, To take a - way trans -
His cov - e - nant re - move; His name shall stand for -

gres - sion, And rule in e - qui - ty.
ev - er; His great, best name of Love.

149 Ewing. 7s, 6s, D.

Anna L. Waring, 1850. — *Alexander Ewing.*

1. In heav'n - ly love a - bid - ing,
   No change my heart shall fear;
   And safe is such con - fid - ing,
   For noth - ing chang - es here.

2. Wher - ev - er He may guide me,
   No want shall turn me back;
   My shep - herd is be - side me,
   And noth - ing can I lack.

3. Green pas - tures are be - fore me,
   Which yet I have not seen;
   Bright skies will soon be o'er me,
   Where dark - est clouds have been.

CHRISTIAN SCIENCE HYMNAL.

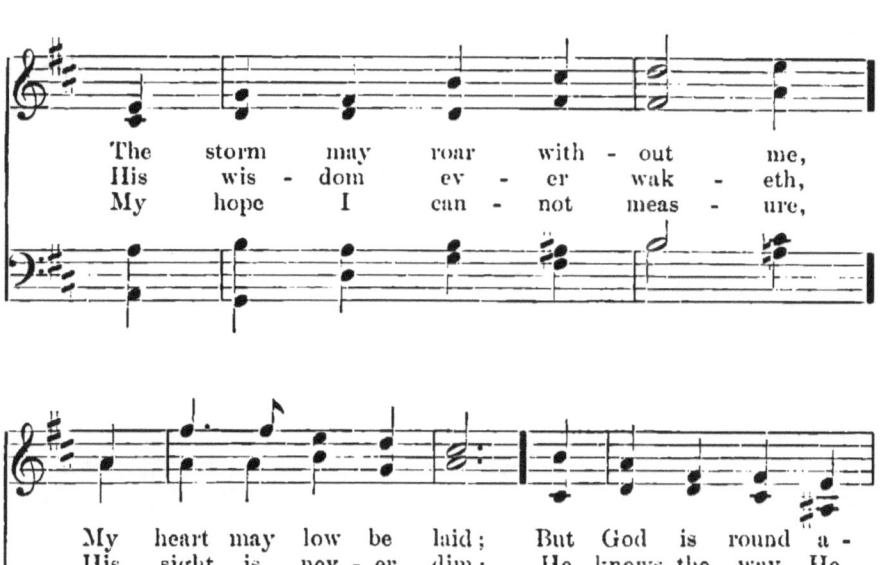

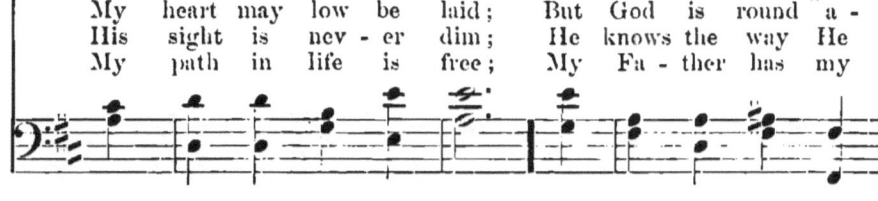

150 Now is the Time Approaching. 7s. 6s. D.

Jane Bortwick, abr.
J. W. Elliott.

1. Now is the time approaching,
2. Let all that now divides us

By prophets long foretold, When all shall dwell to-
Remove and pass away, Like shadows of the

gether, One shepherd and one fold.
morning Before the blaze of day.

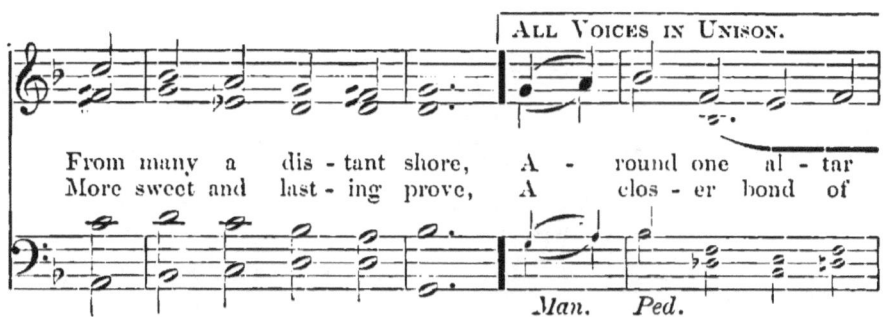

The small notes are for accompaniment only.

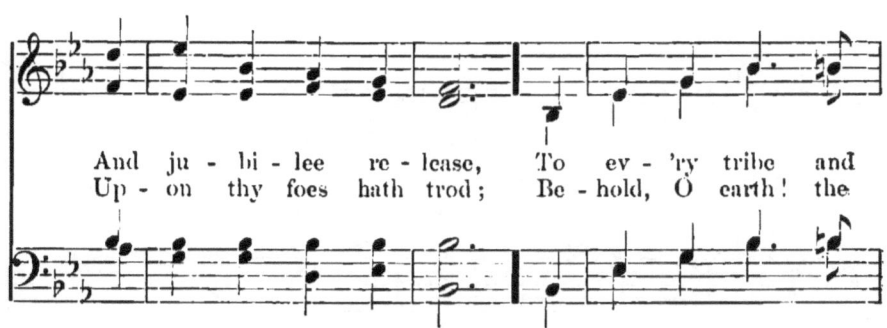

152 God Is My Strong Salvation. 7s, 6s. D.

James Montgomery. Sir John Stainer, M. A., Mus. Doc.

1. God is my strong salvation;
2. Place on the Lord reliance;

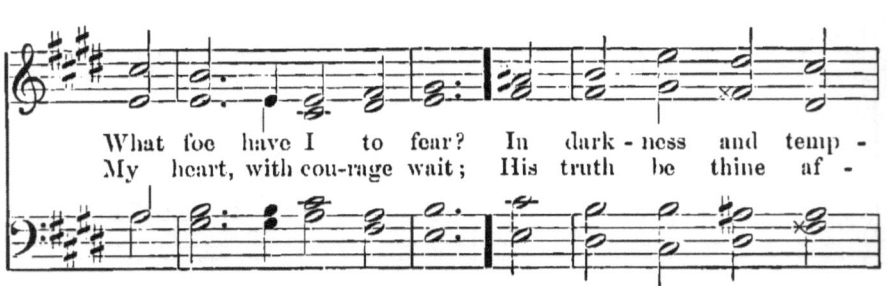

What foe have I to fear? In darkness and temp-
My heart, with courage wait; His truth be thine af-

-tation, My Light, my Help is near:
-fiance, When faint and desolate:

153 Missionary Hymn. 7s, 6s, D.

Lowell Mason.

1. A glorious day is dawning,
   And o'er the waking earth
   The heralds of the morning
   Are springing into birth.

2. The advocates of error,
   Fore-see the glorious morn,
   And hear in shrinking terror,
   The watch-word of reform.

3. The watch-word has been spoken,
   The light has broken forth,
   Far shines the blessed token
   Upon the startled earth.

CHRISTIAN SCIENCE HYMNAL.

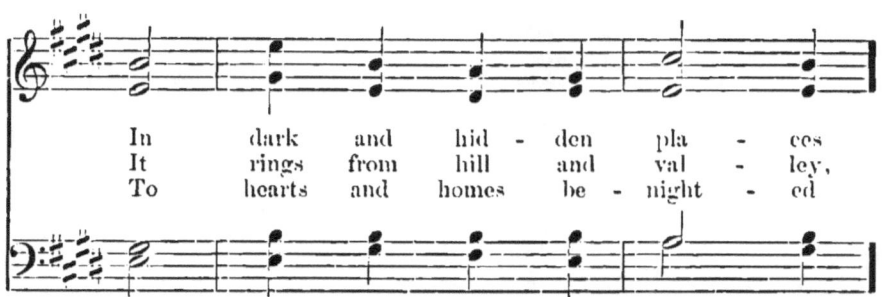

In dark and hid - den pla - ces
It rings from hill and val - ley,
To hearts and homes be - night - ed

There shines the bless - ed light; The beam of truth dis -
It breaks op - pres-sion's chain, A thou-sand free - men
The bless - ed truth is giv'n, And peace and love, u -

plac - es The dark - ness of the night.
ral - ly, And swell the might - y strain.
nit - ed, Point up - ward un - to heav'n.

154 I Know No Life Divided. 7s, 6s, D.

Rev. Carl Johann Philipp Spitta.
Tr. by Richard Massie, alt. and abr.

William Henry Monk. Mus. Doc.

1. I know no life divided, O Lord of life, from Thee; In Thee is life provided
2. I fear no tribulation, Since, whatsoe'er it be, It makes no sepa-

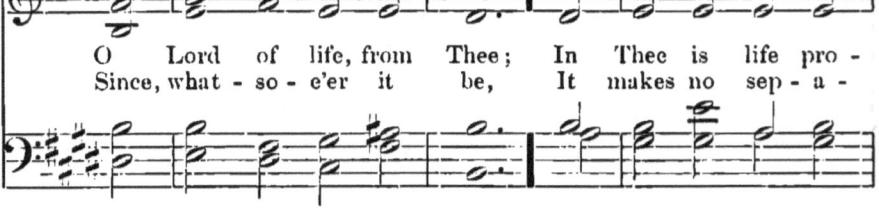

vided For all mankind and me:
ration Between my Lord and me.

CHRISTIAN SCIENCE HYMNAL.

I know no death, O Fa - ther,
Since Thou, my God and Teach - er,

Be - cause I live in Thee; Thy life it is which
Vouch-safe to be my own, Though poor, I shall be

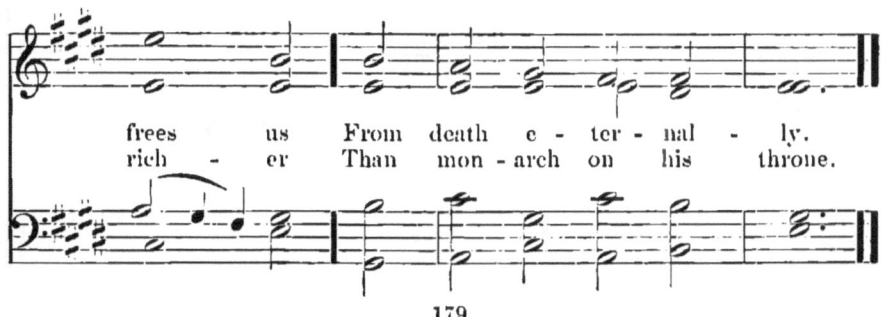

frees us From death e - ter - nal - ly.
rich - er Than mon - arch on his throne.

155 St. Cecilia. 6s.

Kathleen, alt. and abr.
Rev. S. G. Hayne, Mus. Doc.

1. What is thy birth-right, man, Child of the perfect One! What is thy Father's plan For His beloved son?
2. Thou art Truth's honest child, Sinless and pure of heart. Treading, meek, undefiled In Christly paths apart.
3. Dreams of sense disappear As Truth dawns on the sight, The phantoms of thy fear, Fleeing before the light.
4. Take then the charmed rod; Thou art not error's thrall! Thou hast the gift from God— Dominion over all.

157 St. Gertrude. 6s, 5s.

S. Baring-Gould.   Arthur S. Sullivan.

1. On - ward, Christian sol - diers, Marching as to war,
2. Like a might - y ar - my, Moves the Church of God;
3. Crowns and thrones may per - ish, Kingdoms rise and wane,
4. On - ward, then, ye peo - ple, Join our hap - py throng;

With the cross of Je - sus Go - ing on be - fore.
Bro - thers, we are tread - ing Where the saints have trod;
But the Church of Je - sus Con - stant will re - main;
Blend with ours your voic - es In the tri - umph - song;

Christ, the roy - al Mas - ter, Leads a - gainst the foe;
We are not di - vid - ed, All one bod - y we.
Gates of hell can nev - er 'Gainst that Church pre - vail;
Glo - ry, laud, and hon - or Un - to Christ the King;

CHRISTIAN SCIENCE HYMNAL.

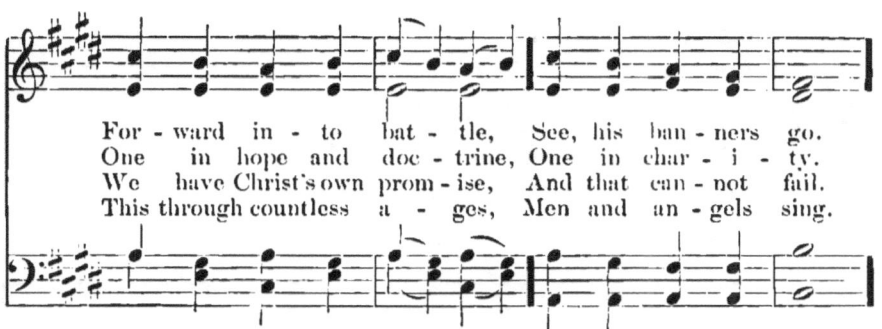

For - ward in - to bat - tle, See, his ban - ners go.
One in hope and doc - trine, One in char - i - ty.
We have Christ's own prom - ise, And that can - not fail.
This through countless a - ges, Men and an - gels sing.

Chorus.
On-ward, Christian sol - diers, Marching as to war,

With the cross of Je - sus, Go - ing on be - fore.

4 Then, with my waking thoughts bright with Thy praise,
   Out of my stony griefs Bethel I'll raise;
      So by my woes to be
      Nearer, my God, to Thee,
   Nearer, my God, to Thee, nearer to Thee.

5 Or if on joyful wing cleaving the sky,
   Sun, moon, and stars forgot, upwards I fly,
      Still all my song shall be,
      Nearer, my God, to Thee,
   Nearer, my God, to Thee, nearer to Thee.

159 Italian Hymn. 6s, 4s.

M. M., alt. — F. Giardini.

1. From out the hid-'ous night, Seeking Thy perfect light, Dear Lord, I come! Ambushed on ev-'ry side, Dark error's foemen hide; Ambushed on ev-'ry side, Thou lead'st me on.
2. Armed with Thy Truth's sharp steel, No fear of foes I feel,— Strong in Thy might. Love, crowning all with peace, Bids strife and tumult cease; Love, crowning all with peace, Makes service light.
3. Turning from death and sin, Thy Life to enter in, Lord, may I prove,—All things to us are giv'n, Health, hope, and joys of heav'n,—All things to us are giv'n, Gifts of Thy love.

160 Truth Comes Alike to All. 6s, 4s.

Brackett.

1. Truth comes a-like to all, Who on Her name dare call,
2. Come, all-per-vad-ing Love, Blest heart of Heav'n a-bove,

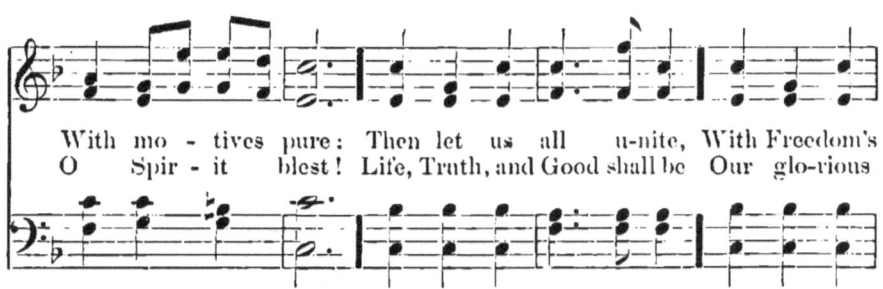

With mo-tives pure: Then let us all u-nite, With Freedom's
O Spir-it blest! Life, Truth, and Good shall be Our glo-rious

star in sight, Press on-ward in the right, Which shall en-dure.
Trin-i-ty. And ev-'ry heart shall see E-ter-nal rest.

161 St. Nicolas. 7s, 5s, D.

Rev. Mary B. G. Eddy.   Wm. Stevenson Hoyte, alt.

1. Shep-herd, show me how to go O'er the hill-side steep, How to gath-er, how to sow, How to feed Thy sheep;
2. Thou wilt bind the stub-born will, Wound the cal-lous breast, Make self right-eous-ness be still, Break earth's stu-pid rest;
3. So when day grows dark and cold, Tear or tri-umph harms, Lead Thy lamb-kins to the fold, Take them in Thine arms;

163 Eddy. 8s, 4s.

Rev. Mary Baker G. Eddy. — Brackett.

1. O'er wait-ing harp-strings of the mind There sweeps a strain,
Low, sad, and sweet, whose measures bind The power of pain;

2. And wake a white-winged an-gel throng Of thoughts, il-lumed
By faith, and breathed in rap-tured song, With love per-fumed.

3. Then His un-veiled, sweet mer-cies show Life's bur - dens light.
I kiss the cross, and wait to know A world more bright.

4 And o'er earth's troubled, angry sea
 I see Christ walk,
And come to me, and tenderly,
 Divinely talk.

5 Thus Truth engrounds me on the
  Rock
 Upon Life's shore,
'Gainst which the winds and waves
  can shock,
 Oh, nevermore!

6 From tired joy and grief afar,
 And nearer Thee,—
Father, where Thine own children
  are,
 I love to be.

7 My prayer, some daily good to do
 To Thine, for Thee,—
An off'ring pure of Love, where-
  to
 God leadeth me.

Copyright, 1897. By permission.

164 St. Vincent. 9s, 8s.

F. A. F., abr.
J. Uglow.

1. In Thee, oh Spirit, true and tender, I find my Life, as God's own child; Within Thy Light of glorious splendor, I lose the earth-clouds, drear and wild.
2. Within Thy Love is safe abiding From ev'ry thought that giveth fear; Within Thy Truth, a perfect chiding. Should I forget that Thou art near.
3. In Thee I have no pain or sorrow, No anxious thought, no load of care. Thou art the same today, tomorrow; Thy love and truth are ev'rywhere.

165 Eventide. 10s.

Henry Francis Lyte, abr.
William Henry Monk, Mus. Doc.

1. A-bide with me: fast falls the e-ven-tide; The darkness deepens; Lord, with me a-bide: When oth-er help-ers fail, and comforts flee, Help of the helpless, O a-bide with me.
2. I need Thy pres-ence ev-'ry pass-ing hour, What but Thy grace can foil the tempter's pow'r? Who like Thy-self my guide and stay can be? Thro' cloud and sunshine, O abide with me.
3. I fear no foe, with Thee at hand to bless; Ills have no weight, and tears no bit-ter-ness: Where is death's sting? where, grave, thy vic-to-ry? I triumph still, if Thou abide with me.

166 Redemptor. 10s.

Horatius Bonar, alt.
Arthur Henry Brown.

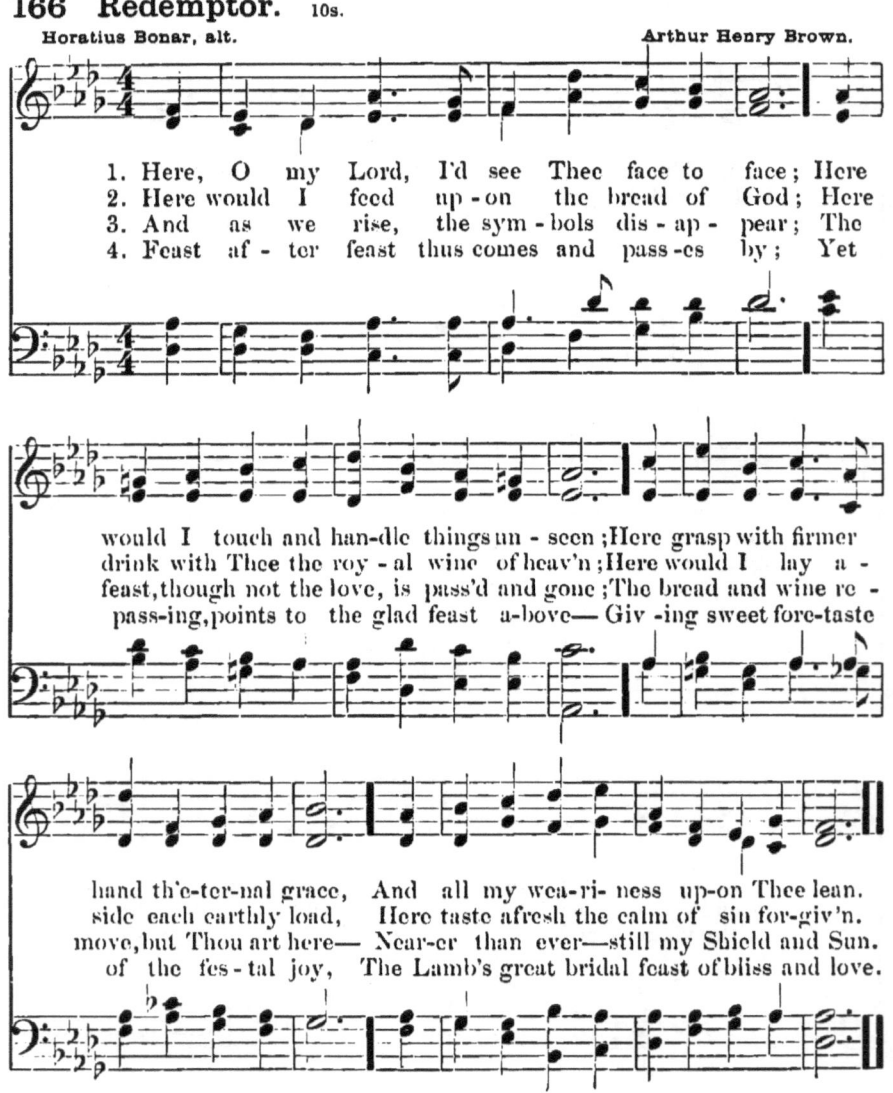

1. Here, O my Lord, I'd see Thee face to face; Here would I touch and han-dle things un-seen; Here grasp with firmer hand th'e-ter-nal grace, And all my wea-ri-ness up-on Thee lean.
2. Here would I feed up-on the bread of God; Here drink with Thee the roy-al wine of heav'n; Here would I lay a-side each earthly load, Here taste afresh the calm of sin for-giv'n.
3. And as we rise, the sym-bols dis-ap-pear; The feast, though not the love, is pass'd and gone; The bread and wine re-move, but Thou art here— Near-er than ever—still my Shield and Sun.
4. Feast af-ter feast thus comes and pass-es by; Yet pass-ing, points to the glad feast a-bove— Giv-ing sweet fore-taste of the fes-tal joy, The Lamb's great bridal feast of bliss and love.

168 Truth. 10s.

Theodore Parker. I. Pleyel.

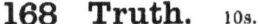

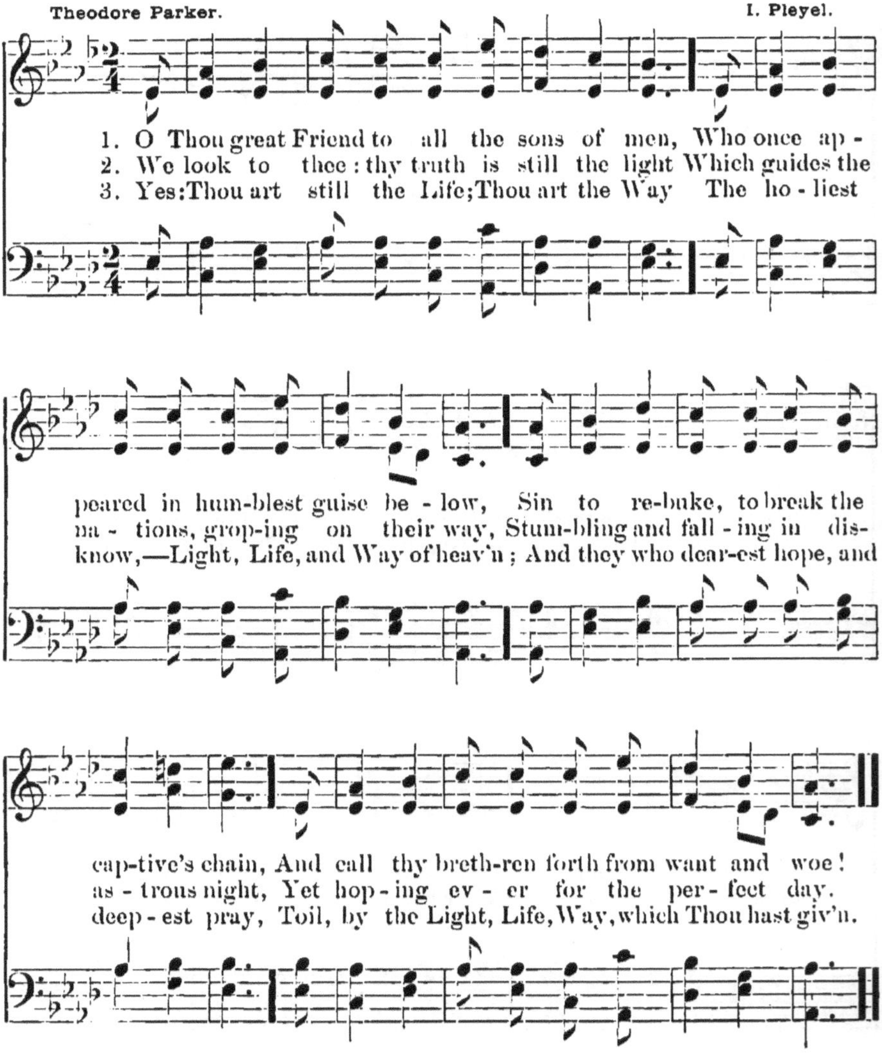

169 Lux Benigna. 10, 4, 10, 4, 10, 10.

John Henry Newman, abr.
Rev. J. B. Dykes, Mus. Doc.

1. Lead, kindly Light, a-mid th'encircling gloom, Lead Thou me on! The night is dark, and I am far from home,— Lead Thou me on! Keep Thou my feet! I do not ask to see . . The dis-tant scene,—one step enough for me.
2. I was not ev-er thus, nor pray'd that Thou Shouldst lead me on: I lov'd to choose and see my path; but now, Lead Thou me on! I loved the gar-ish day, and spite of fears, . Pride ruled my will: remember not past years.

172 Oh, He Whom Jesus Loved has Truly Spoken. 11s, 10s.

John G. Whittier.   Rev. J. B. Dykes, Mus. Doc.

1. Oh, he whom Jesus loved has truly spoken, That holier worship, which God deigns to bless, Restores the lost, and heals the spirit broken, And feeds the widow and the fatherless.
2. Then, brother man, fold to thy heart thy brother! For where love dwells, the peace of God is there: To worship rightly is to love each other; Each smile a hymn, each kindly deed a pray'r.
3. Follow, with rev'rent steps, the great example Of him whose holy work was doing good; So shall the wide earth seem our Father's temple, Each loving life a psalm of gratitude.

173 Lyons. 11s (or 12s, 11s).

Anon.
Francis Joseph Haydn.

1. Be firm and be faith - ful; de-
2. If scorn be thy por - tion, if

sert not the right; The brave be - come
ha - tred and loss, If stripes or a

bold - er the dark - er the night!
pris - on, re - mem - ber the cross!

CHRISTIAN SCIENCE HYMNAL.

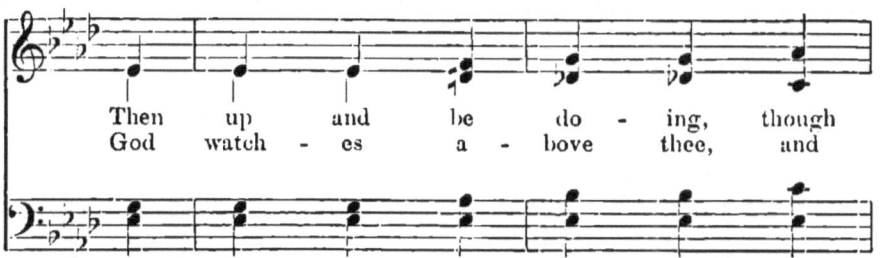

174 While Thou, O My God, Art My Help and Defender.

11s (12s, 11s).

Brackett.

1. While Thou, O my God, art my help and de-fend-er,
2. Yes, Thou art my ref-uge in sor-row and dan-ger,

No cares can o'er-
My strength when I

whelm me, no ter-rors ap-pall;
suf-fer, my hope when I fall,

CHRISTIAN SCIENCE HYMNAL.

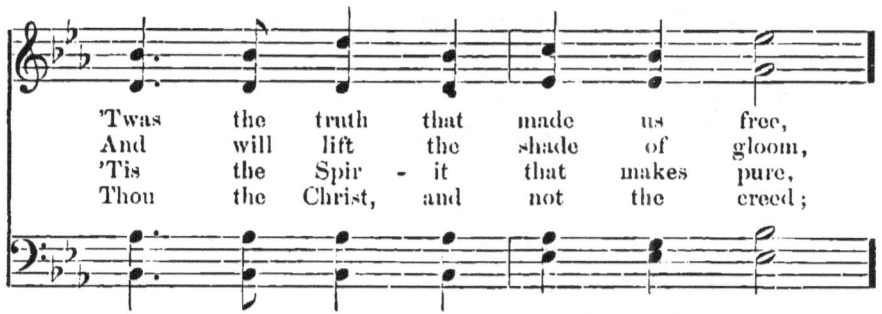

'Twas the truth that made us free,
And will lift the shade of gloom,
'Tis the Spir - it that makes pure,
Thou the Christ, and not the creed;

And was found by you and me
And for you make ra - diant room
That ex - alts thee, and will cure
Thou the Truth, in thought and deed;

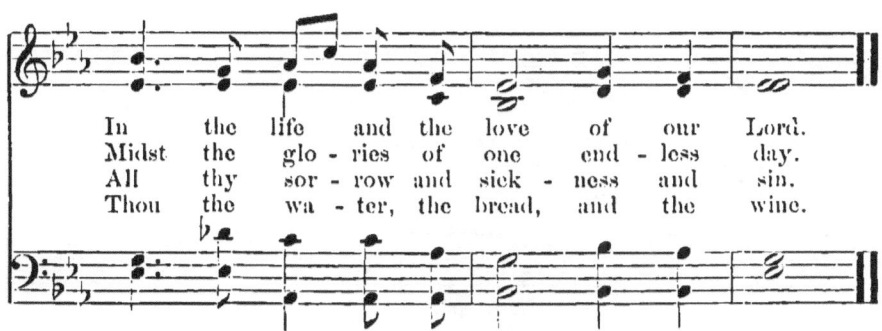

In the life and the love of our Lord.
Midst the glo - ries of one end - less day.
All thy sor - row and sick - ness and sin.
Thou the wa - ter, the bread, and the wine.

179 O'er Waiting Harp-Strings of the Mind. C. M.

Rev. Mary Baker G. Eddy. — Brackett.

1. O'er wait-ing harp-strings of the mind
   There sweeps a strain, Low, sad, and sweet,
   whose meas-ures bind The
2. And wake a white-winged an-gel throng
   Of thoughts, il-lumed By faith, and breathed
   in rap-tured song, With
3. Then His un-veiled, sweet mer-cies show
   Life's bur-dens light. I kiss the cross, and wait
   to know A

Copyright, 1887. By permission.

CHRISTIAN SCIENCE HYMNAL.

```
pow'r    of     pain,    The    pow'r   of     pain ;
love     per -  fumed,   With   love    per -  fumed.
world    more   bright,  A      world   more   bright.
```

4 And o'er earth's troubled, angry sea
    I see Christ walk,
And come to me, and tenderly,
    Divinely talk.

5 Thus Truth engrounds me on the Rock
    Upon Life's shore,
'Gainst which the winds and waves can shock,
    Oh, nevermore!

6 From tired joy and grief afar,
    And nearer Thee,—
Father, where Thine own children are,
    I love to be.

7 My prayer, some daily good to do
    To Thine, for Thee,—
An off'ring pure of Love, whereto
    God leadeth me.

CHRISTIAN SCIENCE HYMNAL.

To where the foun - tains are ev - er flow - ing:
I long have wan - dered for - lorn and wear - y:
Nor an - y tears there, nor a - ny dy - ing:

I'm a pil - grim, and I'm a stran - ger;

I can tar - ry, I can tar - ry but a night.

182 I Need Thee Every Hour.

"Without Me ye can do nothing." JOHN 15 : 5.

Mrs. Annie S. Hawks.   Rev. Robert Lowry, by per.

1. I need Thee ev-'ry hour, Most gra-cious Lord; No tender voice like Thine Can peace afford.
2. I need Thee ev-'ry hour; Stay Thou near by; Temptations lose their pow'r When Thou art nigh.
3. I need Thee ev-'ry hour, In joy or pain; Come quickly and abide, Or life is vain.
4. I need Thee ev-'ry hour; Teach me Thy will; And Thy rich promises In me fulfil.
5. I need Thee ev-'ry hour, Most Holy One; Oh, make me Thine indeed, Thou blessed Son.

REFRAIN.

I need Thee, oh! I need Thee; Ev-'ry hour I need Thee; O bless me now, my Saviour! I come to Thee.

Used by permission of Bigelow and Main, owners of copyright.

183 Shepherd, Show Me How to Go. 7s, 5s, D.

Rev. Mary B. G. Eddy. — Brackett.

1. Shepherd, show me how to go O'er the hill-side steep, How to gather, how to sow, How to feed Thy sheep; I will list-en for Thy voice, Lest my footsteps stray, I will fol-low and re-joice All the rug-ged way.
2. Thou wilt bind the stubborn will, Wound the callous breast, Make self righteousness be still, Break earth's stupid rest; Strangers on a bar-ren shore La'bring long and lone— We would en-ter by the door, And Thou know'st Thine own;
3. So when day grows dark and cold, Tear or triumph harms, Lead thy lambkins to the fold, Take them in Thine arms; Feed the hun-gry, heal the heart, Till the morning's beam; White as wool, ere they depart—Shepherd, wash them clean.

Words copyrighted, 1887. By permission.

184 Shepherd, Show Me How to Go. 7s. 5s D.

Rev. Mary B. G. Eddy. Sir G. A. MacFarren, Mus. Doc.

1. Shepherd, show me how to go O'er the hill-side steep, How to gather how to sow, How to feed Thy sheep; I will lis-ten for Thy voice, Lest my footsteps stray, I will fol-low and re-joice All the rugged way.
2. Thou wilt bind the stub-born will, Wound the cal-lous breast, Make self righteous-ness be still, Break earth's stu-pid rest; Stran-gers on a bar-ren shore Lab-'ring long and lone—We would en-ter by the door, And Thou know'st Thine own;
3. So when day grows dark and cold, Tear or triumph harms, Lead Thy lambkins to the fold, Take them in Thine arms; Feed the hun-gry, heal the heart, Till the morning's beam; White as wool, ere they depart,—Shepherd, wash them clean.

188 Lead, Kindly Light, Amid the Encircling Gloom.

10, 4, 10, 4, 10, 10.

John Henry Newman, abr.   Brackett.

1. Lead, kind-ly Light, a-mid th'en-circ-ling gloom,
2. I was not ev-er thus, nor pray'd that Thou

Lead Thou me on! . . . The night is
Shouldst lead me on: . . . I loved to

dark, and I am far from home,—
choose and see my path; but now,

CHRISTIAN SCIENCE HYMNAL.

Lead . . Thou . me on! . . .
Lead . . Thou . me on! . . .

Keep Thou my feet! I do not ask to see
I loved the gar - ish day, and, spite of fears,

The dis - tant scene,—one step e - nough for me.
Pride ruled my will: re - mem - ber not past years.

189 Nearer, My God, to Thee, Nearer to Thee. 6s, 4s.

Sarah F. Adams. Brackett.

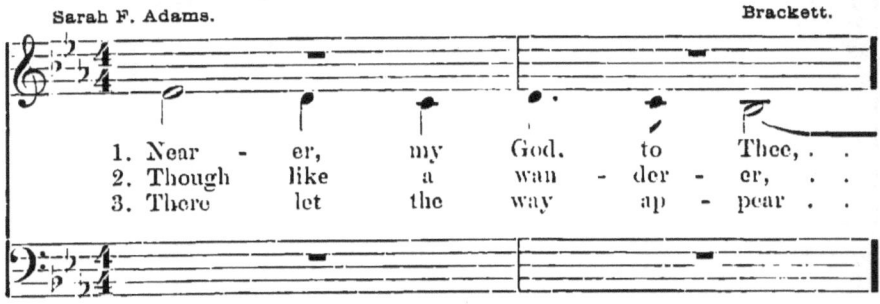

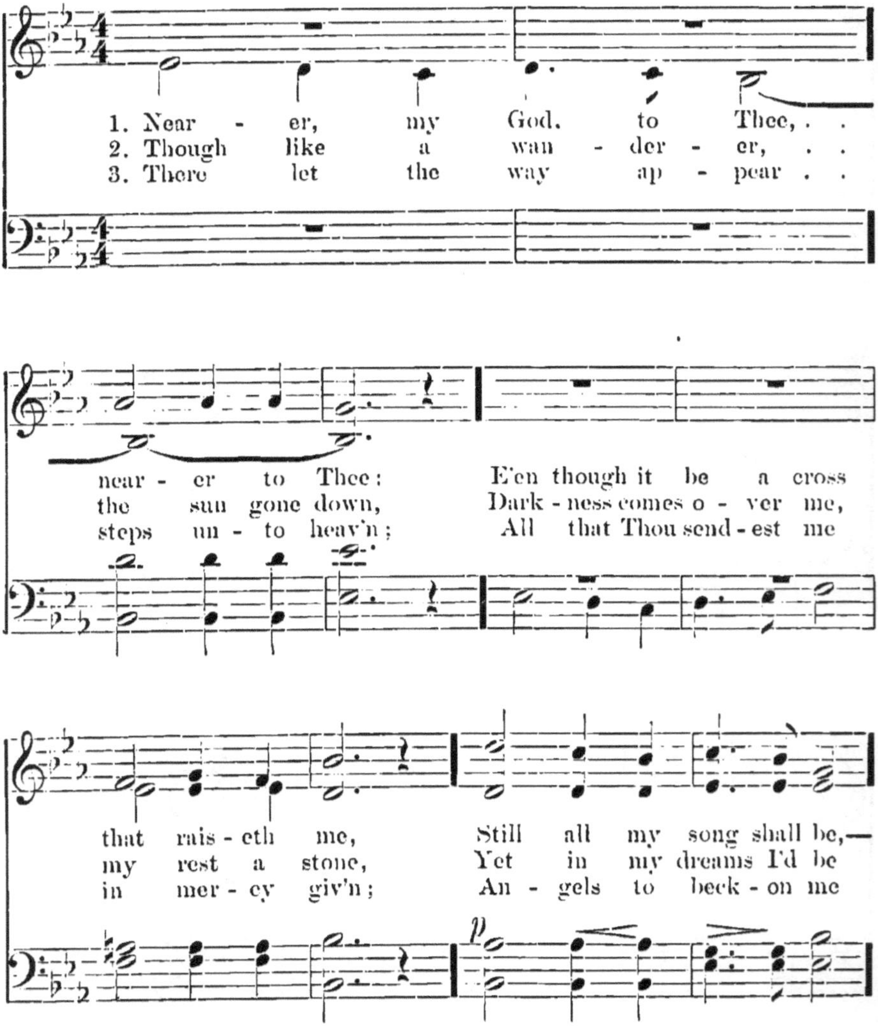

CHRISTIAN SCIENCE HYMNAL.

4 Then, with my waking thoughts bright with Thy praise,
   Out of my stony griefs Bethel I'll raise;
   So by my woes to be
   Nearer, my God, to Thee,
   Nearer, my God, to Thee, nearer to Thee.

5 Or if on joyful wing cleaving the sky,
   Sun, moon, and stars forgot, upwards I fly,
   Still all my song shall be,
   Nearer, my God, to Thee,
   Nearer, my God, to Thee, nearer to Thee.

The small notes are to be sung, but very softly.

190 Rouse, ye Soldiers!

Watch ye, stand fast in the faith, quit you like men, be strong. — 1 Cor. 16:13.

M. H. Tipton.   J. H. F.

Earnestly.

1. Rouse, ye sol-diers of the cross! And put your ar-mor on; Brave-ly fight for truth and right Till vic-to-ry is won.
2. Rouse, ye sol-diers brave and true! Un-furl your ban-ner high! Bold-ly stand at Christ's com-mand, For, see, the foe is nigh!
3. Rouse, ye sol-diers, to the charge! Our Cap-tain's gone be-fore; Grand-ly march with shout and song, Un-til the war is o'er.

Copyright, 1884, by Fillmore Bros. By permission.

CHRISTIAN SCIENCE HYMNAL.

191 God Made All His Creatures Free. 7s.

Montgomery, alt. and abr. — Brackett.

1. God made all His creatures free;
   Life itself is liberty;
   God ordained no other bands
   Than united hearts and hands.

2. So shall all our slav'ry cease,
   All God's children dwell in peace,
   And the new-born earth record
   Love, and Love alone, is Lord.

The small notes are for accompaniment only.

INDEX.

FIRST LINE.	TUNE.	AUTHOR.	NO.
Abide not in the realm of dreams		Dykes	18
Abide with me, fast falls the eventide	Eventide	Monk	165
Abide with me, fast falls the eventide		Brackett	185
A glorious day is dawning	Missionary Hymn	Mason	153
Be firm and be faithful, desert not the right	Lyons	Haydn	173
Beneath the shadow of the cross		Brackett	84
Beneath the thick but struggling cloud		Novello	58
Be true and list the voice within	Linwood	Rossini	37
Breaking through the clouds of darkness	Bavaria	German	127
Bright was the guiding star that led		Brackett	80
Call the Lord thy sure salvation		Dykes	112
Cast thy bread upon the waters		Brackett	116
Church of the ever-living God		Roberts	54
City of God, how broad and far	St. Agnes	Dykes	65
Come, thou all-transforming Spirit	Zion	Hastings	133
Come to the land of peace	State Street	Woodman	97
Come, ye that know and fear the Lord		Brackett	74
Day by day the manna fell	Nuremburg	Ahle	135
Eternal mind the Potter is		Spohr	92
Everlasting arms of love		Brackett	136
Every human tie may perish		Brackett	132
Faith grasps the blessing she desires	Dedham	Gardiner	43
Father, hear the prayer we offer		Brackett	120
Father, my all in all Thou art		Brackett	20
Father, Thou joy of loving hearts		Brackett	10
Fight the good fight with all thy might	Park St.	Venua	13
From all that dwell below the skies	Old Hundred	Franck	1
From out the hideous night	Italian Hymn	Giardini	159
From the table now retiring	Sicily	Sicilian Melody	111
Gird thy heavenly armor on	Vesper	Stainer	162
God comes, with succor speedy		Brackett	148
God is love; His mercy brightens		Monk	114
God is my strong salvation		Stainer	152
God is the Life, the Truth, the Way		Brackett	28
God made all His creatures free		Brackett	191
God made all His creatures free		Foster	144
God's glory is a wondrous thing	Coronation	Holden	45
Gracious spirit, dwell with me	Halle	Haydn	145
Guide me, O Thou great Jehovah		Brackett	134

INDEX

FIRST LINE.	TUNE.	AUTHOR.	NO.
Had I the tongues of Greeks and Jews		Brackett	14
Happy the heart where graces reign		Brackett	44
Happy the man who knows	Silver Street	Smith	109
Hath not thy heart within thee burned		Tours	16
Hear our prayer, oh gracious Father	Stockwell	Jones	117
Heirs of unending life		Brackett	104
Help us to help each other, Lord	Naomi	Naegeli-Mason	53
Here, O my Lord, I'd see Thee face to face	Redemptor	Brown	166
He that goeth forth with weeping		Lloyd	130
He that has God his guardian made	Bera	Gould	39
High in the heavens, eternal God		Garrett	38
Holy Bible, book divine		Brackett	142
Holy Father, Thou hast taught us	Greenville	Rosseau	129
How beauteous on the mountains	Greenland	Psalter	151
How beauteous were the works divine	Federal Street	Oliver	23
How bless'd are they whose hearts are pure	Manoah	Rossini	51
How firm a foundation, ye saints of the Lord	Portuguese	Reading	170
How gentle God's commands	Dennis	Arr. by Mason	93
How lovely are Thy dwellings, Lord	Maitland	Allen	55
How sweet, how heavenly is the sight	Balerma	Wilson	57
How sweetly flowed the gospel sound	Ward	Arr. by Mason	33
I am the Way, the Truth, the Life	Ortonville	Hastings	41
I cannot always trace the way		Brackett	32
I cannot walk in darkness long		Hervey	78
I know no life divided		Monk	154
I look to Thee in every need	Calm	Hastings	176
I praise Thee, Lord, for blessings sent		Brackett	2
I worship Thee, sweet Will of God		Brackett	68
If God is all in all		Brackett	156
If my immortal Saviour lives		Brackett	30
If on our daily course, our mind	Truro	Burney	5
I'm a pilgrim and I'm a stranger		Anon	181
Immortal Love, forever full	Colchester	Purcell	77
Imposture shrinks from light		Brackett	96
In atmosphere of love divine	Southport	Kingsley	81
I need Thee every hour		Lowry	182
In heavenly love abiding	Ewing	Ewing	149
In Thee, oh Spirit, true and tender	St. Vincent	Uglow	164
In Thee, oh Spirit, true and tender		Brackett	186
It came upon the midnight clear	St. Asaph	Giornovichi	89
Jesus, what precept is like Thine	Germany	Beethoven	7
Joy to the world, the Lord is come	Peterborough	Harrison	47
Joy to the world, the Lord is come		Lahee	64
Kingdoms and thrones to God belong		Brackett	6
Know, O child, thy full salvation		Bach-Steggall	118
Lead, kindly Light, amid the encircling gloom	Lux Benigna	Dykes	169
Lead, kindly Light, amid the encircling gloom		Brackett	188
Let party names no more		Brackett	98
Look, ye saints! the day is breaking	Weimar	Ancient Melody	131
Lord, I have made Thy word my choice		Brackett	70
Lord, may Thy truth upon the heart		Schumann	12
Lowly in heart to all who sought	Eckhardtsheim	Zeuner	87

INDEX.

FIRST LINE.	TUNE.	AUTHOR.	NO.
Make channels for the streams of love		Brackett	86
Make haste, O man, to do		Brackett	110
Mighty God, the First, the Last	Hendon	Malan	137
My feet shall never slide	Lischer	Schneider	175
Nearer, my God, to Thee	Bethany	Mason	158
Nearer, my God, to Thee		Brackett	189
Now is the time approaching		Elliott	150
Now sweeping down the years untold	Science	Brackett	121
Now to our loving Father, God	Evan	Havergal	59
O for a faith that will not shrink	Belmont	Mozart	67
O God, whose presence glows in all		Brackett	26
O Life, that maketh all things new	Missionary Chant	Zeuner	3
O Lord, I would delight in Thee	Brattle Street	Pleyel	91
O Love Divine, whose constant beam		Barnby	34
O Love! O Life! our faith and sight	Simpson	Spohr	71
O Lord, where'er Thy people meet	Hursley	Monk	25
O, my people, journeying onward	Autumn	Marecchio	125
O pure Reformers! not in vain	Dundee	Franc	83
O Spirit, source of light	Thatcher	Handel	95
O Thou great Friend to all the sons of men	Truth	Pleyel	168
Oh, be not faithless! with the morn		Brackett	177
Oh, do not bar your mind	Olmutz	Arr. by Mason	107
Oh! ever on our earthly path		Sangster	52
Oh, he whom Jesus loved has truly spoken		Dykes	172
Oh, not alone with outward sign		Brackett	90
Oh, sometimes gleams upon our sight	Woodworth	Bradbury	17
Oh, speed thee, Christian, on thy way		Brackett	56
O'er waiting harp-strings of the mind		Brackett	163, 179, 180
One cup of healing oil and wine	Rockingham	Mason	35
One holy Church of God appears	St. Martin's	Tansur	85
On the night of that last supper	Wilmot	Weber	119
Onward, Christian Soldiers	St. Gertrude	Sullivan	157
Onward, Christian, though the region	Bartimeus	Jenks	113
Our God is love; and all His saints	Avon	Wilson	73
Our God shall reign where'er the sun	Ware	Kingsley	9
Our heaven is everywhere		Brackett	94
Partners of a glorious hope		Brackett	138
Peace be to this congregation		Brackett	128
Planted in Christ, the living vine		Brackett	66
Prayer is the heart's sincere desire		Dykes	88
Press on, dear traveler, press on		Monk	40
Press on, press on, ye sons of light		Brackett	4
Rouse, ye soldiers of the cross		J. H. F.	190
Saw ye my Saviour? Heard ye the glad sound	Communion Hymn	Brackett	178
Scorn not the slightest word or deed	Oaksville	Zeuner	48
Servants of Christ, arise		Brackett	102
Shepherd, show me how to go	St. Nicholas	Hoyte	161
Shepherd, show me how to go		MacFarren	184
Shepherd, show me how to go		Brackett	183
Soldiers of Christ, arise	Boylston	Mason	103
Sow in the morn thy seed		Brackett	108
Speak gently, it is better far		Brackett	60

INDEX.

FIRST LINE.	TUNE.	AUTHOR.	NO.
Still, still with Thee, when purple morning breaketh.	Henley	Mason	171
Still, still with Thee, when purple morning breaketh.		Brackett	187
Sun of our life, Thy quickening ray		Brackett	8
Supreme in wisdom as in power	Azmon	Arr. by Mason	61
Take up thy cross, the Saviour said	Duke Street	Hatton	27
Teach me, my God and King		Brackett	100
The Christian warrior, see him stand	Hebron	Mason	31
The God who made both heaven and earth	Coventry	English Melody	79
The hopes Thy holy word supplies		Brackett	22
The lifted eye and bended knee		Brackett	36
The loving Friend to all who bowed		Smith	82
The morning light is breaking	Webb	Webb	147
The Spirit breathes upon the word		Brackett	42
Theories which thousands cherish	St. Sylvester	Dykes	123
They are slaves who will not choose	Herford	English Tune	143
They who seek the throne of grace	Dijon	Ger. Evening Hymn	141
Thine is a living way	Laban	Mason	99
Thou art the Way, to Thee alone	Heber	Kingsley	75
Thy will, almighty Father, Thine		Wesley	24
'Tis God the Spirit leads	St. Thomas	Tansur	101
To us a Child of Hope is born	Christmas	Handel	69
True, the heart grows rich in giving		Haydn	126
Truth comes alike to all		Brackett	160
Upon the Gospel's sacred page	Zephyr	Bradbury	15
Vainly, through night's weary hours		Brackett	124
Wait, my heart, upon the Lord		Brackett	140
Walk in the light! So thou shalt know	Peterborough	Harrison	63
Walk with your God, along the road		Smart	76
Watchman, tell us of the night	Watchman	Mason	146
We may not climb the heavenly steeps	Arlington	Arne	49
We say to all men far and near		Brackett	46
We walk by faith of joys to come		Brackett	72
Well for him who all things losing	Rathbun	Conkey	115
Whatever dims thy sense of truth		Brackett	50
What is thy birthright, man	St. Cecilia	Hayne	155
When God is seen with men to dwell	Wareham	Knapp	21
When Jesus, our great Master, came	Hamburg	Arr. by Mason	29
When like a stranger on our sphere	Retreat	Hastings	19
While Thou, O my God, art my help and defender		Brackett	174
Why is thy faith, O child of God, so small?	Berlin	Mendelssohn	167
Why search the future and the past	All Saints	Knapp	11
With Love and Peace and Joy supreme		Dykes	122
Word of Life, most pure, most strong	Pleyel	Pleyel	139
Ye messengers of Christ		Oakley	106
Ye timid saints, fresh courage take		Brackett	62
Ye servants of the Lord	Athol	Harrison	105

www.ingramcontent.com/pod-product-compliance
Lightning Source LLC
Chambersburg PA
CBHW031745230426
43669CB00007B/493